Elder Story 2
Who We Are

Compiled and Edited by

Gordon A. Long

AIRBORN PRESS
Delta, B. C.

ElderStory 2
Who We Are

Published by

Airborn Press

4958 10A Ave, Delta, B. C.

V4M 1X8

Canada

ISBN: 978-0-9952687-7-7

Printed by CreateSpace

Cover Design by Tania Mendoza

Cover Photo Vadim Ivanov

Other Books in This Series:

ElderStory 1: Who We Were
Available at amazon.ca

Coming Soon

ElderStory 3: More Tales – Fall, 2017

For the Families

This is a book of real stories about real people. ElderStory has requested that, wherever possible, storytellers get permission from people to use their names and stories. The stories remain the intellectual property of the storytellers. It is our hope and desire that no one will be hurt or offended by his or her portrayal in any of these tales.

For the Storytellers

These stories as published may not be exactly the same as the story you usually tell. It is the nature of folk tales that they change over time. You tell the story differently each time. People remember it differently. In the process of recording/transcribing/editing, things get changed, especially if there is translation involved. But the story is still your story, and it is a story that people want to hear.

Thanks To

John Lusted and the KinVillage Association in Tsawwassen

Morgan Gadd, for his expertise and support.

Staff, students and families of Ecole Woodward Hill Elementary School, especially Lisa Anderson, Ravinder Grewal, Jas Kooner, Kelly Mcquillan and of course Elaine Vaughan, who organized our sessions.

Staff, students and families of Surrey Central Elementary School, especially principal James Pearce, and Sean Austin, John Kovach, Kevin Larking and Grace Jackson.

Staff and residents at the Langley Lodge Care Home

Pamela Chestnut, Mona, Tania Mendoza and Mercedes at DIVERSEcity.

Introduction

The ElderStory Project came about in a very natural way. So many people deeply regret not making a record of their family's stories before it was too late. And so those stories died with the people who told them.

Those of us on the Surrey Seniors Planning Table looked for a way to keep family stories moving down through the generations. It is good for children to know where they came from, who their families are. It leads to a sense of belonging and a stronger sense of self worth.

So we sought ways to enhance the telling of stories to keep family members and communities in contact with each other. And the ElderStory Project was born, with the intention of bringing the generations together through storytelling.

Our storytellers come from all walks of life, from all ages, from many cultural groups. Their histories originate in communities in rural Canada: in small villages in India and Iraq: in large towns and big cities around the world. But wherever they originate, the message always comes out the same. "Now we are here, and much though we love the places we came from, in this place we are happy."

The Surrey Seniors' Planning Table and DIVERSEcity Community Resources Society hope that you will enjoy these very Canadian stories.

Contents

1. A Dangerous Time

1. Tom Brown – Thrown From the Car

My wife worked in New Westminster before we got married. She lived up beside us out on 72nd, and she would come out on the weekends to home, and Sunday night I would drive her back to New Westminster, where she stayed for the week. We were about half way in to Vancouver and there were some Americans up here, I guess one American and one Canadian, and they were racing.

I had a 1927 Durante at that time. I guess we were puttering along about 20 miles an hour. They were telling me afterwards they were doing over 80 miles an hour. And they ran right into the back of us.

Luckily, they hit hard enough, and it collapsed the car, and that bowed it out and shot us out the roof. The roof on those, there was iron up to the top, and the roof was canvas covered in the centre, and I guess it exploded away, because it shot the two of us out of the car and across the ditch, and across the fence into the pasture.

Lucky it didn't hurt, although June had a sore neck for a long time, and I had a cut on my head. But when it first happened, I thought I was back overseas, because I'd tried that trick a few times over there, driving over landmines. Same thing. The explosion, I guess, makes you lose consciousness, because I don't remember, and June doesn't remember going over the fence. Because when I woke up of course with her, she was saying, "Why are we here? What are we doing out here?"

And then finally I came back to the road, and I had to get through the fence in the dark, and there was one light, not very

1

bright, hanging on it, there was a red taillight quite far down because the car, I guess it shot in the ditch and it skidded down the road on its side.

The guys in that car were drunk because I climbed up on the car and all I could hear was moaning. I hollered down, "Are you okay? Is anybody hurt?"

"And the driver said, "Yes, we're okay, we're just stalled, leave us alone."

I said, "You're not okay, there's somebody hurt down there."

They said, "No, we're okay."

Lucky there was a house fairly close, and the owner heard the noise and he came out to look, and he came down finally and he had a light. It was dark and we couldn't really understand what happened and what was going on. There was more confusion than anything else there.

2. Jack Lillico – Lost Needle

I was doing a big magic show on the third of January 1949 in a house in Shaughnessy. Claybourn was the name of the people. Claybourn Brick Mills, out in the Valley, you know. And they had a huge party that they wanted me to entertain for. So halfway through the act I did what I call swallowing needles. You take a length of thread and pop it in your mouth and drink some water, and you take these 20 ordinary steel needles and put them in your mouth one at a time and flip them back on your tongue and drink the water, and eventually you pull out the whole thread with the needles all threaded on.

I have to tell you how the trick goes because this night it went wrong. When you work this trick, you have a load in your left cheek with the points back and the thread running through in the front of your mouth. When you flip the needles back, they stick together as a lump with your saliva, and you roll it over to the right side. You can only work if for about 15 minutes and it gets agitating, and that warns you when to do the trick, half way through your show.

I was downstairs getting my cheque for the show and I took the needles out of my mouth, the single needles I'd put in. And

I generally counted them, and there was one missing. I thought I'd swallowed it.

First of all when I discovered that I did this the two nurses came down dressed in white that looked after the kids in the home. They gave me bread to eat. Of course I could swear I swallowed the needle.

So I phoned Brock Fahrni, who if you know Shaughnessy hospital there's a Brock Fahrni Building down there, and he and I owned a Star Craft boat together at the yacht club. I said, "I've swallowed a needle." So I had to meet him at about 11 o'clock down at the General Hospital.

When we went down to the hospital, he got an esophagus specialist and they took X-rays, and they said, "We can't tell whether you swallowed the needle or not because of the bread." The recommendation was to go home and have oatmeal and castor oil.

I never had the castor oil. I ate enough of the cereal for seven guys. But we went back and vacuumed the place, but we never found the needle. I don't know if it was a miscount, or what happened, or whether I swallowed the needle or not.

It was an embarrassing situation. You never work that in a kid's show. You only do it for adults.

3. Gordon Long – Science Lesson

I was about 10 years old, I guess, and this is where I learned my first lesson about physics. Brian Anderson and I – Brian was the nephew of the lady that lived next door – we were playing one day down at the foot of their driveway, which is about a quarter of a mile from our driveway, and this was before Highway 16 was paved. It was pretty muddy in the spring, and we were unsupervised and young and stupid, and we were throwing mud at the wheels of the cars driving by on the highway, thinking this was all sorts of fun, but drat it, we could never hit them.

Because every time we'd throw at the wheels, by the time the mud ball got there, the car was gone.

Well, Gordon being the scientific type, I did some thinking, and I thought, "What I really need to do is throw the mud ball ahead of the car, and the car will get there and the wheel will get there just as the mud ball gets there." Very intelligent.

I timed it absolutely perfectly, except for the altitude of my shot, and the mud ball that I threw hit dead centre of the windshield of the car.

The car came to a sliding halt in the mud. And I went pelting up the Palling road, which was the side road that went up into the community, and unfortunately Brian went pelting up the road to his aunt's place.

I cut through the gravel pit and headed home, but unfortunately Brian went home and the owner of the car of course knew exactly where to go, and he drove up there. Brian told them it was me, so the guy drove across to my house, and by the time I got home, there he was standing in the yard yelling at my mother.

So I listened to that, and then I went up to another neighbour's house and I played there for the afternoon, but sooner or later I had to come home. I got into more trouble for that escapade than I ever got into in my life. And it was all because I learned a science lesson.

4. Allan Brown – The Pickup

When they were logging above the road at the back end of the cut-block, trees that they couldn't buck would break loose and come sliding down. They'd run right across their road and right across our road and sometimes take the road out.

The trouble is that you can't always tell where it's gonna go.

I went up the road in the morning to where we were blasting, and it was a fairly new pickup we had. I had a helper when I was drilling because he changed the steel. So I told him to take the crummy down and put it in the switchback and park it there. Usually he stayed there and had a coffee or something, but this time he came right back up. Lucky for him.

Finally the faller came down, and "Al," he said, "I've got a little news for you. Take a look; your pickup is no more." One of the big trees got loose and came sliding down right on top of the pickup and just flattened it. When they fall them usually they come down. If they happen to turn and get started and away they go.

It was a fairly new pickup, and the company I worked for wasn't too happy about that.

5. Jamie Long – Dick Carroll Hill

The Dick Carroll Hill was the access into the Palling community from Highway 16, and it was a pretty steep hill. I used to like to walk up to the top of the hill and then I'd get on my bike and then I'd gun it down the hill, full speed ahead, with the cardboard-and-clothes-pin clickers on the wheels that went "dr-r-r-r-r" as I went.

So I'd go up the Dick Carroll Hill and I'd give 'er, runnin' down there goin' "dr-r-r-r-r" all the way down. But I kinda forgot that there was traffic on Highway 16. So I went gunnin' out right in front of a salesman. Boy, I'll tell you he nearly clipped me. It was really close. And I only had a few hundred feet to get to my own driveway. I was goin' so darn fast, and I go gunnin' in there, and he came after me, and I went behind the house, and he was right after me. Boy, I'll tell ya. He got ahold of me and he shook me like crazy, yellin' at me. Oh, it was a scary darn thing. I never did that again, let me tell you!

Gordon Long

To add to that, when I was about 10 years old a friend of mine, Gordon Worthing, that lived in Decker Lake, rode his bicycle down their driveway and out on the road in front of a car and got killed. I was a pallbearer at his funeral, so I'm glad, if I have to say it, I'm glad it was him and not you.

6. Darryl Catton – Driving the Ambulance

After the military I went back to Ontario. I walked straight into a job as chief engineer at the hospital in Huntsville, Ontario. I had a little help from my father and some board members, and the administrator was a friend of ours.

So I did that for 13 years, and they came to me one day because the ambulance service in town, the guy had quit and they wanted someone to drive temporary, so they said. So they asked me if my men could drive ambulance, and the orderlies would be the attendants. So I agreed to that. That was a big handover, losing patients and everything else.

We didn't have proper ambulances; it was just a truck they had made into an ambulance to keep the stretcher inside in wintertime. One of the first jobs we got was to go pick a guy up, and they lived on a hill. Now the ambulance attendants they were orderlies usually, but the local undertaker's son was also an attendant. Now you'd never get away with the things we got away with. We weren't qualified.

So I had to go down and find him, and they had a hardware store – that was another business – and get him over there, meanwhile the guy's dying, you know. And we got over to this house, and it's on a hill.

This is a true story. It sounds like I'm embellishing. I've told a lot of people and they don't believe. You can tell in their eyes.

So I'm driving, and I just want to get back to the hospital.

Normally the operator, the driver, isn't supposed to get involved, but you do. You can't help it. So anyhow we go in and the guy's out of it. We had to put a straight jacket on him. He's flopping all over. We took him out and Bob, the undertaker's attendant, pushed him in. The ambulance normally had a clamp on the side. You pushed them in on a stretcher, and there were clamps. But this is a makeshift thing we made up, so we just pushed it in. It was dark, and we were on top of a hill, and I ran around the front and jumped in and Bob goes in the passenger side and I hit the gas, and we were at the top of the hill. I heard a clunk and turned around and the doors flew open, and there goes the patient. It was pitch black. Luckily it was just a shallow ditch. So we're out there with flashlights trying to find the patient. He was out of it; he didn't know what was going on. He slid down into this little ravine, and we were trying to find him.

We got him and put him in the ambulance, and Bob got in and held on to him until we got to the hospital. Well, as soon as we opened the door, this guy threw up. You can imagine the mess. He just slid out. It was a small town, and we knew everybody. I talked to the guy later, but I never did tell him.

They had a party for me when I left the hospital, and I told the administrator, "I gotta tell you a story." And I told her.

She said, "Darryl, I'm glad you didn't tell me that at the time." This was years later. "We coulda got sued."

So I have a lotta stories about the ambulance. I could write a book alone about the ambulance. We didn't have radios when we first started out. They'd phone in, and they'd just tell you where to go. Most of them were false alarms. I got fed up with them because you're away from the hospital in a far house, and in a hospital that size you have patients where you have to be there at certain times. You can't just walk out.

And you're going way up in the park, up lakes in a boat in the middle of the fall and freezing to death, handling drunks, so I gave it up. So eventually they did get in an ambulance.

7. Sandy Long – A Winter Stroll

This was a visit to our neighbours that went wrong when I was very young. We were down at our new house at Palling, on Highway 16; it was just being constructed in 1949, and I think I was just turned three. I announced to Mum that I was going to visit the Carrolls. Carrolls lived about a quarter of a mile towards Decker Lake, east along Highway 16.

She wasn't watching me, I guess, when I went out the driveway. I had said Carrolls, but I knew deep in my heart that I was going to Eklunds, about a half a mile west on Highway 16, so I turned the wrong way, going to Eklunds.

I walked almost a half a mile on the crust of the snow. It was late winter, and we had great access to the bush at that time of the year because of the crust that would form on the snow after a cold night with a previously warm day. Anyway, I got to Eklunds' fences and cross fences in their barnyard. The house sat a little bit back from the highway, and of course I took the easiest way, which was a shortcut, and I got hung up in a barbed wire fence, and there I was, stuck.

Fortunately Carl Swanson Junior came along the highway in his old Model B Ford Pickup, and he spotted me out in this field stuck in the fence, and he came out to get me. But there was about three feet of snow and he was sinking through the crust. He finally got me free, and then apparently – I don't remember this quite so well –apparently I ran away from him and he couldn't catch me once he got me free.

But he finally caught me, kinda guessed who I was and took me back home. He figured I was one of the Long kids. I remember riding back in his truck.

8. Tom Brown – Crash on Vedder Mountain.

We were logging up at the top of Vedder Mountain, and my Dad wanted to move down to the bottom, so we loaded up in the evening in the back of the truck hauler, and progressed down the road. I guess it was must have been dark, and the driver stepped on the brakes, and the red tail light came on and it shone up through the platform. Alan saw the red light and he started screaming, "Fire, fire, fire!" because he thought it was on fire.

Jesse, the driver, heard him screaming, so he stopped the truck and came running back to see what was going on, to see the fire. I guess there was no brake; he just left it in gear and it started rolling forward. He ran back to get in, but Mum was sitting in the cab with our sister, Mary, who was quite young at the time, on her lap. It was straight over the bank on her side, so she decided she was going to get out the driver's side.

So she was pushing and hollering at Jesse to "Take the baby, take the baby!" but he wanted to get in and drive the truck. Finally he got ahold of the steering wheel so that it ran into the bank and stopped, but that was lucky, because if it would have gone the other way, we would have all gone down the bank. It was pretty steep there, and it would have rolled a time or two, and it might have killed a few of us. I don't know, but I was glad we didn't have to try it.

9. Sandy Long – A Wild Ride

Some of those trucks Dad had. No brakes, time and time again. They were hydraulic brakes in those old Fords dating in the early '50s. The four-ton, Dear John, was a '51.

(Ed. Note: Mum named all our vehicles. Dear John was the same bright green colour as a John Deere tractor. Also, a "Dear John" letter meant bad news. If a guy overseas during the WWII got a "Dear John" letter, it meant his girl back home had chucked him over for someone else. The other truck was the Pink Elephant; that name speaks for itself. It was a 1950, I think. It was older and even less reliable. Mum had a sharp sense of humour, and she hated those trucks.)

The chains on the tires would break and the loose ends would whip around and tear the hydraulic lines off. So Dad fixed the brakes from time to time, but for large periods there were no brakes on the trucks.

I have to tell the story about Dear John when we were towing the mill down the Palling Road with the Caterpillar D-2 bulldozer. That was one of the near misses of my life.

Dad was working on his homestead, which was up at the back end of the Palling community, three or four miles back from the highway, and we lived down on the highway. He had been doing some cutting on his own property that winter, and then breakup came and he was done, so he was going to move his Bellsaw sawmill that was on a Model A truck frame. He could just tow it behind the bulldozer.

So he was walking the dozer down the public road with the sawmill behind it. And behind that, came Sandy at age 12, driving Dear John, and on the back of the lumber truck was Gordon and Sigurd Esplin. Sigurd didn't drive. He was a fairly well off Norwegian fellow who just loved the work in the bush, and he loved the work around the mill, and when there was nothing much happening around the Decker Lake Forest Products planer, he worked for Dad. And he was helping us with this move.

And it was the boringest job, because Dad would be walking the Cat ahead and I'd be waiting, and then I'd start up, and I'd upshift, and I'd get it into second or third, and very quickly I'd catch up to Dad, and then I'd pull over and wait for Dad to get ahead a bit. Stop and go. Stop and go. Very, very slow.

And there's a big hill called Carroll's Hill on the East Palling Road coming down to a T-junction with Highway 16. I was a bit apprehensive about this hill because there were no brakes on the truck.

That's right. No brakes on the truck and a 12-year-old kid driving. I knew what it was all about, but I was still apprehensive. So we got near the top of the hill, just starting to be a slight down pitch, and I thought, "I'd better downshift into bull low, so I can go down the hill on compression, and shut off the key if I want to stop."

Needless to say, I missed the shift. And all of a sudden I'm in neutral. I'm revving it up, and I knew enough to double clutch, but I couldn't get it back into gear.

"Turn off the key! Turn off the key!" Sigurd is shouting. "Turn off the key!"

But I knew there was no sense in turning the key off because I had no connection with the rear tires; there was no hold-back on the motor any more. So I put it in the ditch on the left-hand side of the road. On the right-hand side of the road there's a real gulch, and I'd have killed somebody if I ran it all the way down to the highway.

But I didn't. I put it into the ditch, and there was a berm on the other side of the ditch, and we stopped on top of the berm.

So I went down and told Dad. "I ran off the road." I told him what happened.

"Aw," he said. "You would have been all right in second."

Which was true. I kinda knew I'd be all right in second, but I wanted to be safe. But I should have downshifted when I was on the level and then crept down. I made a mistake there. But that could have been fatal for somebody. As it was Dad just got into the truck backed it out on the road and went down the hill.

But if I'd left it for another two seconds I would have been in serious trouble, but I did the right thing, given that I'd made the mistake in the first place.

I was also on a much more serious runaway...I think it was Pat Ford with us. (Ed. Note: Pat Ford is the name of the logger. Dear John is the name of the truck. Which was a Ford. No relation, I'm sure.)

We were in Dear John; I can remember that as clear as anything. I was 8 or 9 years old. We were up past the main camp quite a ways; there was a road with a steep side-cut that went up a big hill, and then Dad had a tie sale at the top.

It was in the evening and we were coming down the hill with a full load of ties, and it was muddy, muddy, muddy, with deep ruts. The whole road was ruts.

Dad had been grinding along on a relatively flat area in the cut-block, and then he got out on the main haul road. The truck had a two-speed rear axle, so he up-shifted into high range. We broke over the ridge of the hill and started down and all of a sudden. "Kapink!" We already had no brakes, and we now had no connection to the back wheels. So when the compression came on instead of it lugging along through the deep mud it started to coast, and then it popped out.

So all of a sudden this truck's running away, and it's at night. Pat jumped out, and I'm the one in the middle of the seat. You shouldn't really jump out, but he did. There were no doors on the truck at the time, and no fenders, because then you could see not to run into things in the bush. We had a full load, a couple of hundred ties on the back of this truck with no brakes.

Dad curved it into a brush pile on the down side of the road. The upper side was a cut bank, and if you went up there, you'd roll it. So he carved it and hit it perfectly, and we came to a stop. Pat came running up.

We walked back to camp in the dark. Dad said, "I think I know what happened. I think that two-speed axle didn't shift right, and it popped into neutral."

So we went back the next morning and he fired her up and put her back into low range and backed it out on the road again, and down the hill we came, no harm done.

Oh boy, oh boy, that could have been fatal, though.

2. Wars of the World

1. Joyce Schmaltz – Fish and Chips.

You have to be English to understand this. I was in the military police during WW II, and I don't know why but lots of times I had the same shift, the one where the boys were going off to Europe, and they would go through Waterloo station.

One night in the blackout with the bombs and everything I happened to be down there when I saw a friend that I'd been out with a couple of times, a British boy. His regiment was going.

"Oh, Joyce!" He comes and gives me a big hug and knocks my hat off and oh, my goodness, we had a fight to find my hat in the dark and everything. But anyway I found my hat, and we went into a corner and had a little kiss and a cuddle.

And he hugged me and he said, "I'm going to tell you something that I want you to remember all your life."

So I thought, "Oh, yeah, here comes he usual stuff about that he loves me, you know, and when I get back..."

So then he gave me another hug, but this time he put his nose sort of quite near my head, and he said to me, (so I was waiting for this big love thing,) and he said very nicely, "You always smell of fish and chips."

I've remembered that all my life!

The reason for this is because during the war we could not get shampoo so we washed our hair with Sunlight soap that my mother washed the clothing in. So then you took vinegar – in England we didn't have anything but malt vinegar – so you put the vinegar on your head to get rid of all the scum and stuff from the soap. So after you put the malt vinegar on, then you put water on to wash the vinegar out.

Well I did this once a week. I never knew that I smelled of vinegar. Here he was so lovingly saying, "I'm going to tell you something that I want you to remember all your life. You always smell like fish and chips."

So I rushed home as soon as I could get off duty, and I said to my Mum, "Gee, do I smell like fish and chips?" And she said, "Yes."

I loved the fish and chips bit instead of saying he loved me because he was going away, never knowing if he was coming back. I've never forgotten that.

2. Maggie Gooderham – World War II

When the war broke out my school was evacuated to the country, but my parents didn't want me to go, so I left that school at about 17 and I took a secretarial course so I had something to do. My parents were okay with that. It was something I could do that I could work with. So I became an accomplished secretary.

We lived in a town called Guildford. It was quite small in those days, of course. It's hard to imagine. We had no cars or anything. We had to put our cars up on blocks in the garage. We kept the distributor cap somewhere different in case the Germans invaded and had access to a bunch of cars because they couldn't drive without the distributor cap. It seems strange, now, to have no cars. It sounds silly, but my sister and I loved our car. We had a Daimler, and it was up on blocks, so she and I used to sit in the back and play cards, because we liked being in the car. It sounds silly, but at the time we liked it.

People didn't realize quite how close we came to losing the war, you know. They'd taken over the whole of Europe, and Greece and Norway, and most of North Africa.

I remember Dunkirk. After that, everybody in England expected to be invaded, and they would walk right over us. My dear father joined the Home Guard, and they used to drill with broomsticks. Nobody had any weapons of any kind in the country. They could have walked right in. But Hitler made that stupid mistake of invading Russia instead. It was absolutely idiotic.

And Dunkirk. At the time we regarded it as a great victory, because a call came out over the BBC, "Would anyone with a small boat go to Dunkirk and help to rescue everyone that made their way to the beach." So all these little boats made their way to Dunkirk, and they picked about 300,000 men, which at the time we thought was a huge victory, which it was. It was also a big defeat, but at the time, rescuing all these Poles and French and English; to us it seemed wonderful.

I remember my mother saying that the church bells would all ring if the invasion started. And one night she came upstairs and said to my sister and me. "Get up girls, the invasion has started." Of course it seemed at the time as if it was so possible. We got up and packed a case of absolute nonsense. Nothing useful. Photographs and useless things. Then we went downstairs and listened to the radio, and it must have been a false alarm. But at the time it seemed so desperately real. It was frightening because at the time it was so believable. Which it was, of course.

But if it ever happened again, I wouldn't go out on the road. I'd die in bed. It seems a much better idea. Of course we don't know at the time.

When the school decided to evacuate to the country, my parents didn't want me to go. So that's when I took the secretarial course.

3. Maggie Gooderham – Egypt

The war was going so terribly badly at the time. The Germans had taken over most of the world except the States. So all I wanted to do when I was old enough was to join up and do my tiny little bit to help.

So when I was 18, I joined the Air Force. This was a bit of help, but I felt it was my duty and wish to help more. I was in the Air Force two or three years and then the call came out. They wanted volunteers to go to the Middle East because of the war In North Africa. The whole place was getting taken over by the Germans. The allies made their last stand at a place called El Alamein. And we had the first victory there since the war started, so it was a wonderful place to be.

The girls went over there to release the men to fight. So we just did the technical side while the men won the war. But it was the turning point of the war. The first victory we had because the Germans were favoured by the Egyptians. Most of them wanted Germany to win. The Egyptians didn't like the British. A lot of the Egyptians had German flags ready to wave, but they were disappointed, of course.

The first time I was in Egypt about a year.

After the Armistice was signed, I was doing some private work for a man who lived in Kenya. He was going back to start a safari outfit, and he liked my work, so he said if ever I wanted to go out to Kenya he would pay my way. Which would be very nice.

I took my demob in Egypt. When we first went home to England, the rationing was still on. It was worse than during the war. We had very small rations. One egg a month, I remember. But the nice thing about when the Americans came to England they had huge amounts of everything, of course. So we liked to ask them to dinner, and they would bring huge steaks. Ooh. Enough meat to do us a month. Of course they didn't realize how little we had. They had so much that some of the people resented them. The humblest man in the Air Force would drive a huge car and the station commander would have an Austin 7; that's just an example of how much they had of everything. They would dish out almost anything you wanted. They had chocolates, cigarettes – I didn't smoke at the time, but yes, cigarettes – and everything.

But other than that life was so terribly dreary in England. Rations were so small, and the weather was awful, so I thought, "I'm going to take him up on the job in Kenya."

So I said I would like to come, and he wired right back. "Booked you on such-and-such a ship." And so in a matter of weeks I was on my way to Kenya. Which was much nicer than life in England, you know.

After I was there for, oh, a year or so I met my first husband. He was in the Air Force also, and he was doing a survey of the countryside. He finished that, and he got the Air Force Cross for doing it, he did such a good job. We agreed we would get married, so he had to go back to his base in Cairo, and then he came back and we got married in Nairobi. He had to get back, because he was stationed in Cairo, so I went back to Cairo for the second time.

Being a civilian that time was not nearly as nice as having a uniform to protect one. Quite different. So after a while we went back to England and I'm sad to say he got killed in a plane crash. So I had two small children by that time, 4 and 2 years old, which was at the time quite devastating. I could never understand at the time why God allowed him to be killed, because he was such a good father and husband, but we don't know what lies ahead, so we have to accept it.

4. *Maggie Gooderham – Scorpion in Egypt.*

We all lived in tents, and everything was in a tent, and I went to the washroom tent one day, and there was this huge scorpion.

I looked at it, and I said, "Oh, I can't kill it, my foot's too small." So I looked around and took the lid off a garbage can and clumped it over the scorpion. And it just sat there. And I said, "What am I going to do?"

So I went outside and called the guard in. He was a British soldier. I said, "Under that lid is a scorpion. I want you to kill it."

He said, "How do I do that?"

I said, "Well, you've got big boots, step on it."

He was very unwilling, but I said, "I'll count to three and then lift it up, and then you stomp on it."

So we agreed on that, and I counted to three and of course the scorpion was just sitting there, probably dazzled by the light. Anyway, he stomped on it and killed, and that was the end of that.

5. *Maggie Gooderham – Egypt After the War*

The first time I was in Egypt about a year, and then as a married woman I was there probably another year. The uniform was a protection because the Egyptians were not nice people.

But then I went back again as a civilian, which was different, because with the uniform one had a certain protection. As a civilian of course you were fair game for anybody. In fact it was awful. Everywhere they were always firing guns into the air, just for fun. When my husband was on duty at night, which was often, unfortunately, I used to have a Very pistol under my pillow as a safeguard. Fortunately I never had to use it, but it was nice to have it there.

The first day my husband went back to work after we got back to Cairo a large policeman came to the door and insisted I come down to the police station with my passport.

I said, "I'm not going."

He was a huge man, and he said, "You have to come!"

I said, "I'm not coming with you."

Anyway, he went away, but that was the type of thing they would do all the time. I was glad to get out of that.

My husband used to go to work quite early and he would always say to me, "Get up and lock the door after I've gone."

And I would say, "Oh, yes, dear," and go back to sleep.

And then one day I was lying there, and I heard the door open, and then I heard silence, and then feet shuffling on the floor. I thought, "Ooh, what am I going to do?"

Nothing. I didn't see any weapons. And then he came shuffling to the door, and then it slowly opened and it was my husband. And he said. "I told you to get up and lock the door."

Of course after that I did, but at the time it terrified me, it really did, the way he did that slow shuffle. He was really quite bad. But it certainly taught me a lesson.

6. *Joyce Schmalz – Vignette from WWII*

Wasn't it odd how we met?

"Destiny," you said.

I literally fell into your arms when we smacked into each other. We were going round a corner in opposite directions, heads lifted to the sky, cheering the Hurricane fighter planes doing the "Victory Roll." Then I looked at the twinkle in your eye and your lovely grin. I cut my lip on a brass button on your uniform, and it began to bleed.

Most of the time we had together was a few snatched hours here and there on the top of a double-decker London bus – at the back, whenever that seat was vacant. There we could talk, whisper, laugh, hug and kiss. It was the only place we could be alone; we knew there wasn't much time.

My lip never seemed to heal. I was so sorry afterwards that we didn't have the photograph taken that you wanted so much. I said, "later," because of my lip.

You wanted a lock of my hair because you said it smelled so nice. I said you smelled like an old wet dog when your army uniform got damp in the rain.

I have never forgotten that evening in Waterloo Railway Station. So many troop trains leaving, and so many young people. So crowded, and yet so private. Saying goodbye, trying to be brave and pretending to be cheerful. There wasn't much left to say; we'd said it all on top of buses, and sometimes sitting on a park bench in the blackout.

Your face was wet when I kissed you. I tasted your tears as you did mine. I never saw you again.

I haven't forgotten.

7. *Tom Brown – The War Years*

When I got out of school I started working with my Dad. He was working up on the Hope-Princeton Highway, below the slide, hauling shingle bolts. At that time you could get a call-up for the army and I got mine. So I came to town and reported in. I could have got out because I was in logging, but I thought

"Maybe I'll stay in." It was December, I guess it was. They took me back to Peterborough.

When I arrived back in Peterborough for basic training. I thought at that time I was just going to stay in reserve. When you got called up you didn't have to go overseas, you could stay in Canada.

Before I went overseas, – and that's one of the reasons I went active – I wanted to be a mechanic.

They told me that I didn't go far enough in school, and I talked to them and they said, "You have to have the education." But they said, "You can do it by correspondence and work at night with a crash course and get the training."

Which I did. It was good. I got real good mechanical training.

So I woke up one morning and I had signed up for active duty. They took me to Petawawa for active training, and then I went overseas.

We went over on the Mauritania. There were three ships, the two Queens and the Mauritania that could go over direct without battleship escort. All the rest went in convoys. But we went over direct and zigzagged all the way.

We were set down in the hold in the bottom of the ship where they store stuff down there, and we had to get out and pack our food down in that hole there, and everybody was sick and throwing up, and it was quite a trip. Little did I know I was going to face MUCH worse in the next few years.

But then we got to England, and it was a while before the invasion, so we stayed there and did lots of training. Like my brother Allan, I didn't get too far in school because we had to work to support the family. So more education was welcome. It was good, and I got really well trained as a mechanic.

They wanted to waterproof the tanks for the invasion so that they could keep their heads above the water, so we worked on that quite a bit.

Anyways finally I went in on the invasion in France and went from there up to Belgium and we were up in Germany when the war ended. I was in the Second Anti-Tank Regiment.

But actually it didn't work out. We towed 18-pound guns behind a quad.

But every time they called on us to shoot a tank, the Germans they had their gun was so good, and it could shoot twice as far as us, so we didn't have a hope. It was lucky I was the driver, but when you get close enough, you gotta stop, the guys bail out, get the gun ready. I had to get the truck out of the road to a safe spot, and they had to turn the gun around, spread the legs and try to aim.

The Germans had better tanks than us, and they were blowing us away. So every time we went into action it was gone. So then they took us actually, we were in a Valentine tank for a little bit. It was just about as bad. It had the gun out the back of it. There was a little bit of armour on the side of it, and on the top, but it was the same, you had to try and turn the tank around.

So then actually we got a Sherman. It was better, a little bit, but we still had to plan our routes to find the enemy, try to destroy them before they got us. And we learned, by that time, that no, we couldn't drive down roads and stay out, because we couldn't get close enough to the German tanks to do anything, and even if you did, they were so designed, you know the bullets just bounced off them, so you had to pretty much get on the side of them if you're going to do any damage to them.

There were land mines everywhere. At first the Germans made ones that if you stepped on it you blew up. Then they started making ones that would shoot up in the air and explode, killing all those around.

So that's about all I did during the war was get down on the ground, get in a trench and stay there. They were usually filled with water, and it was scary trying to figure out if it was safe to come out. That was the safe place. If you got down in the ground you were okay as long as you didn't come out.

For almost a year and a half we were in Niemegen, and I don't remember being inside a building. There were some bombed-out houses and barns, but they weren't safe to sleep in. We lived in the trenches and only had dry rations, powdered stuff and horrible old pieces of meat sometimes. The food and conditions were dirty, slim and barely sustaining but somehow I lived. Many, many didn't, and I try not to think about it.

It was pretty awful for a long time after coming home – nightmares, visions, guilt. I was lucky I had a big family and my wife's family, and there was always someone around and things to do, so I didn't get much chance to sink into depression. Family is everything.

8. Dennis Horgan – WWII in the Channel Islands

I grew up in Jersey in the Channel Islands during the German Occupation. The Germans were good to us. That year they had a twin calves on every cow. So my Dad registered one with the Germans, and the other one he stuffed in a secret room in the hay pile. So we had beef and rabbits to eat. He raised his own rabbits.

Old Dad being from Ireland and growing up through the bad times, he figured this out. He'd go in and shampoo a chicken, wring its neck, and in the manure would go the chicken, and down to the manure pile. At night he'd pick up a couple of chickens and save them. But finally he had to clean out the chicken house with a German armed guard all around him.

He used to milk the cows, and the Germans couldn't figure out where all the milk was going. Some of the boys had medicine bottles. They milked the cows into them and threw my Old Man some cigarettes. So we had these cigarettes and free milk. Then one day a fellow Irishman stole his rabbits. Didn't go over too good.

9. Olena Chemeris – Germans in Ukraine during WWII

My Mum was five when WWII began, and her sister was six. At the time they lived with their grandmother in a small village in Ukraine. This village was under occupation by the Germans. German soldiers were billeted in houses in the village, and Ukrainian women would take care of these soldiers. They would cook, they would feed, they would clean they would do laundry.

And it's very interesting and very unusual, but from what I've heard about these soldiers, they were actually really nice to the people they lived with. They would share their food. These little girls wanted sweets and chocolate, and these guys would give them chocolates. They would finish a can of sweetened condensed milk and give the empty can to the little girls, and they would clean it with their finger and lick it off. When I talked to my Mum, that's what she remembers. She remembers these nice things from the German soldiers.

10. Darryl Catton – Air Force

I joined the Air Force in 1956. I went straight from St. John's Quebec where I was in Basic Training, and I went straight to Trade School. I had a trade at 17 before I joined the Air Force, so I was put straight in with the #2 CMU construction crew run by the RCAF. I don't know if you're aware, during the war they had 8 Construction & Maintenance Units. These were construction crews that went around and built the plan. You know the plan for training all the Commonwealth.

So they had to go around and build in record time, build all these buildings and hangers. The #2 CMU was the last one left after the war was over. We went around and rebuilt runways and did all kinds of jobs.

One of those jobs we went to Alert. You know where Alert is? Not Alert Bay. Everybody says Alert Bay. Alert is the last point of land on North America on Elsmere Island. It's 400 miles from the geographic North Pole, not the magnetic.

I was 17 when I was sent up there with 26 guys. We went to Thule, Greenland, first. All the building supplies for Alert were being brought up by ship, and they couldn't get up any farther because of the ice pack, so they dropped them off at a big American base called Thule, and left them there for two years.

So we went up in 1956 and landed, all single men, myself included. We stayed in Thule while the married men went up to Alert. We had to load all this big stockpile down on the docks onto 124 American Globemasters. They had a contract. We didn't have big enough planes. We did that 24 hours a day, back and forth, flying 900 miles to Alert.

And then after that stockpile was diminished we went up to Alert and started helping up there. There were 26 of us, and we had one building. One building. There was a DOT there, the United States Weather Bureau, but they didn't have any Air Force installation. We were told that it was a weather station, which it was, but its main purpose was that it was a listening post. In 1955 they had just released not too long ago that's what in fact it was.

So we weren't prompted about what we were to expect when we got there. They'd built one building. In 1954 a crew had gone in there and put one building up, but they didn't do anything with it. So we were all housed in that one building, 26 of us. I have pictures here of the barracks. The beds are side by side. You couldn't crawl out the side; you had to crawl out the end of them. There was one little room at the end for the cook; that was his room.

I called it the Waldorf Astoria. And there's socks hanging from the ceiling right down in your face. But there was no spit and polish, and we had no papers. The plane came in maybe every two months, if it got in, and we didn't have any connection with the outside world, except we did get a ham radio set up after maybe a month or so.

They had patches to phone Toronto, and Toronto gets on the phone and calls wherever, and you sit in a big room, and you're trying to talk to your wife, and it's sometimes personal, like you're missing her, and you wanna tell her, and these guys are all sitting there with a big smirk. And it's all "over, out" and she doesn't know that, and she's talking away when you're trying to talk. And you've got a certain time, because they have whiteouts out there, and this big fog bank would come in and all the communications cut right out.

In fact, the Russians flew over once; believe it. During the Cold War, they flew over the base at Alert to get communication to find out if we were all right, because one whole week we didn't communicate. Now that's hard to understand, because that created an international incident.

So when we got up there it's total isolation, but it's also the only place on earth where you can get away from the sound of the diesel and look right over, like we're right on the point of land of North America, and it's four hundred miles across to the pole. I used to go up there and sit there and meditate. It's a religious experience to do that. It's hard to explain.

And smelling grass. You know you smell the vegetation, but up there, there's no vegetation, and we didn't realize it until we got out to Edmonton, but the sweet chlorophyll smell was making us kind of bilious. It's hard to believe but that's the truth.

But of course, there's no women, and there's no trees, so they say there's a woman behind every tree. I was there for 6 months at one stretch and didn't come out. I was in Resolute once for nine months and never came out.

So we were in Alert for 6 months and one of the jobs we had to do up there was move graves. I didn't personally; I was working in a team, but the crews come in at night, a small crew, and they all talked. Nobody knows the true story about those graves.

We had to move the graves because a crash occurred two years previously and they were all burnt to death. They didn't have a runway. They had a runway along the ice parallel to the shore, but it was all broke up because it was spring, so they took a Lancaster, and they flew in a load of pipe and other things on board, and pushed it out the back, but a pipe caught around a stabilizer and pulled them into the ground and it exploded.

But that was before I was there. Nine of them were all cremated. So they just put a picket around them and brought in people from Resolute to check it out, and then they had a service, but trying to get bodies into the ground up there? The story was that there were nine guys but only one casket, but that's not true.

But anyhow, they tried to take the bodies out, after they were checked by certain people, and they brought a plane in, an amphibious Canso, where there was open water along the shore, came up onto the shore, loaded the bodies, went down on the water, took off and hit an ice floe and banged up the plane. They turned around and re planted them.

Then in 1957 when we went up we had to move them because we were widening the runway. So we had to take them all up and move them and put them down where they are to this day. They were still there in 2008. But there were 8 bodies. They made rough boxes from the weather station boxes they brought their cylinders up in. So they found the one casket, and they thought the project was finished, but we started scraping the ground, and we found another one, and another one and another one. So we put eight markers up, and they're all there today. But I don't know if they're all in single graves, or if they put them all in one box, and just put 8 graves up.

I talked to some guys who were there in 1955 when it happened. They were in their 90s, so I've got reams of stuff here, trying to get to the bottom of it, When I went up in 2008 I tried to talk to some people up there, about it, but they just know about the basic story about the plane crash, they don't know about it.

Anyway, one of the things we had to do was widen the runway and put in the roads and put up 8 buildings, all prefab buildings. They go up in a couple of days. In the high winds they had two buildings blow down. The eaves stick out and the wind got under the eaves and flipped the lids off. Didn't take the whole building down. So they sent a crew up to fix them. Instead of putting new panels on top, they just took the chainsaw, put a line down and cut the eaves right off. That was so they could get out of there.

Those buildings are gone, now. When I went up in 2008, you could see where they sat, but they're all gone now. They just took them down two years before. My name is up on a board that we all put our names up. One of the guys I talked to said they made up some tables for outside, you know, wooden tables, and probably the names are on one of those tables.

But it was total isolation, and there could have been a war. People don't know. They talk about the DEW line. The DEW line is 1500 miles south of where we were. If they came over the pole like they expected them to, the first place they would bomb would be Alert. Because that's where all the communications was. They were monitoring it. Even in 1957 there were submarines going under the ice, and they put transponders through the ice and they were doing in '57, so this isn't something new. So they would have bombed and we wouldn't have known anything about it. It could have been the Third World War, and we wouldn't have known. Total isolation. But it was an experience of a lifetime and I'll never forget it.

11. Daryl Catton – 45-Gallon Drums

When we first moved up to the Arctic we had no facilities. We had the one building, 26 guys, we had a big back house, or toilet, just outside, and it had a heater in it and it had two 45-gallon drums in the bottom. And then they had panels at the back to pull out. Because there's heat in that building the snow would melt and so the whole building kept sinking lower and lower. And then to get the 45-gallon drums out, you had to go up a little bit of a ridge.

Now those drums, nobody wanted to take those drums out, because it was heated. You can imagine 45-gallon drums of "effluent," you can imagine how sloppy it would be. But every week they'd put up an assigned s**t detail. Your name would be on it. That's where that expression came from.

When it was your turn to go down, you had to get a Cat and a stoneboat, and you had to get those barrels. Most guys just clamped the lids on and rolled the barrels out and set them there and put new ones in. They didn't take them down to the dump.

There was an article came out; they were trying to clean up all the Arctic, and you know all these barrels, and you're wondering where they came from. Well in those days, 45-gallon drums were the means of getting fuel oil for all the vehicles. They didn't have the bladders they've got now. Now they pump it into a bladder and suck it out. Then, it was 45-gallon drums.

So they are all over the Arctic. They never rust because things don't rust. So they line all the roads going down to the villages, and they use them for all sorts of things, including effluent barrels.

So I go out, and here there's four of them. Sitting there. And the Sergeant said, "You've gotta get those all down to the dump."

Now this article I mentioned recently, they couldn't figure out how these dumps are down in Dumbbell Bay, they call it. I know how they got there. I went out there, I had a couple of native guys helping me. You try to roll a 45-gallon drum up an incline. It's heavy to begin with: 450 pounds maybe, and rolling and it's ice and snow. So we get them up to the Cat, and just try to lift them on the stoneboat.

When we were resupplying Alert out of Thule, I was never very big or strong, but we had to put six of them on a pallet to get them out of the bay, and we couldn't get forklifts in because of the snow, so we had to roll them. You tried just keeping them level. I could not lift them up on that pallet. But we had a big guy who could lift them up. Six of them, you'd go underneath the plane, and you were allowed a hundred of them on a plane

We went down to the big cliff that goes right down to Dumbbell Bay, so I'm ready to push these off. The corporal said to me, "The cook is missing one of his garbage pails, but stuff is not easy to get up here. Go down and get it."

So I go down and it's a steep incline, and the Arctic Ocean is down there, Dumbbell Bay, so I'm going down, and he pushes off the barrel. If you watch a barrel going down a slope; it doesn't roll straight. It goes one way and then another. And then the lid fell off..

Well I could just see them sending a letter to my mother saying, "Darryl was killed in action. See the epitaph, 'Killed by the s**t barrel.'"

And I never found the pail for the cook. I went back up and gave the corporal heck. They could have killed me. But they did get the pail back eventually.

So that's how those barrels got down there.

Until they got the buildings up and then they had toilets and plumbing. But those barrels are still there. When I went up in 2008, you could still see barrels. They're all over the Arctic. It will take years to clean up the mess. The Americans left a lot of stuff there, too.

12. Brenda Casey – Yom Kippur War

My mother came to visit me in Israel, just after her anniversary on September 28, so I think she must have arrived about the 30th, and she was staying with me. We were out for dinner on October 6 and the lights went out, but the lights always go out. You've always got power outages; it was a young country; you're used to it. You go out on the street and there's military walking around with machine guns. It's a curious thing to have a young girl with her handbag and little gadgets like Garfield hanging off her handbag, and then her machine gun hanging off her other arm.

But there's all these military people walking around, and then there was a bus with military kids getting on the bus, and my mother was asking about them. In Israel you're in the military from 17 on.

We were taking a taxi home. I lived in a valley and the valley was a very undeveloped area, a new area, but it was a nice apartment.

But there was a roadblock set up at the beginning of my valley. Having learned my Hebrew, in Israel you have to be quite aggressive in the way you spoke to people. Being a polite Canadian was not the norm.

I had people abuse me, one of the reasons I didn't like the country initially, abuse me all the time for being polite and courteous. To get on the bus, you had to use your elbow. You brace your elbow so you can grab the bar on the bus and your elbow is the other way so you can get in front of somebody else. There's no lineup. There is now, but there wasn't in those days.

So this army person comes to the window of the cab and says. "What are you doing here?"

I said, "I live here. What are you doing here?"

He said, "There's a war on."

I said, "There's always a war on. This is Israel. What do you want from me?"

"No, there's truly a war on."

I said, "I work for the News Desk. I would know if there was a war on."

And he said, "Where do you live?"

"I live in that building over there."

He said, "You go in there and you phone your boss and you tell him there's a war on."

So I get to my apartment and my friend with whom I was flatting, said, "They've been calling you all night to go to work."

I said, "What the...?"

"There is a war on. Here's your gas mask and..."

So I had to get another taxi to take me back and argue with the guy at the roadblock again.

So I got into the office, and yes, there was a war on and we were doing our work and my poor mother was just beside herself. She was very scared, and I felt aggravated with her for being scared. She's coming to Israel, and she knows that's the kind of country it is, and I felt aggravated at her for getting frantic. I said, "As soon as I know what's going on I'll call you."

There were no cell phones, so I'm at the office of the Voice of Israel, and I'm working and they tell me, "There's no time to call your mother."

I said, "No, no, she's here. She's at my apartment and she doesn't know what's going on and I have to call her and tell her."

When I phoned she said, "I put on the television." She got the news, some of it in English.

So I told her what was going on, and she said, "Well, do I have to fly home?"

I said, "It's up to you. I'll talk to you when I get home."

The man with whom I'm still friends was one of the first people to cross into Egypt at the front of the lines going through the Sinai, and the man that I was dating then who was the social worker was a bomber pilot, and you're only allowed to call your closest relatives, your partner or your wife.

It was a very sobering thing to be in a country that was so organized for war. They knew exactly what to do. They had the gas masks ready in everyone's apartment, they had the roadblocks set up, they were so militarized, easily, that it felt almost normal other than the blackouts and the news was always focused around the war.

When I was working at the Labour Department, I would go back, and every fifteen minutes there's news, and you would hear everybody run – and it's all women – everybody running down the hallway to where the radios are every fifteen minutes.

It was impressive, I have to put that out there, it was quite impressive, but coming from some place like I had come from it wasn't something that I expected. It was a learning thing to be there.

In Israel when you're pregnant, you make sure everybody knows you're pregnant the minute you're pregnant, because that meant, at that time, you have a child that will be in the military and will fight for Israel. And girls and boys all fight for Israel from 17 to 21. So when I said that we had only girls, secretaries and people that would be in the administration all running to the radio, all their husbands and brothers and fathers were fighting. If you're in the reserves, you're also called up.

It was organized within hours.

The war didn't affect me because they never got into Jerusalem. The only way in which it affected me was that my dear friends Sri and Ben and certainly the people I worked with were always reporting in from where they were. Ben got personal messages in to me about once a week. It lasted about three weeks, I think.

My mother ended up going home to Canada. She got out. Interestingly my friend Ruth was in England at the time, and when she was getting on a plane, there were Israelis fighting to get on the plane. They'd overbooked the plane, and they wouldn't get off. They were holding on to each other. People wouldn't get off the plane, because they wanted to get back to Israel, to be there.

I don't know if that would happen in other places, to fight to get to a war.

I know it's not the same, now, because even when I went back in 1990 it was the beginning of the Infada, and the Gulf War was on, and Sri's son was a paratrooper, and he said, "You know, I don't want to die for my country. I want to live for my country. I've had enough of war." He was a young man.

13. Ghidaa – Refugee Story

We left Nineveh in 2006 because the terrorists told us to leave, and we went to Karakesh, a small city in the north of Iraq. We stayed there for 8 years until ISIS came in 2014, and then we left Karakesh and fled to Erbil. I sold my jewelry to buy clothes, and we left everything else behind, including 2 cars. In Erbil we were in a stadium with 500 people on the bottom floor and 500 people on the top floor and only two bathrooms.

That was in August. After 40 days in the stadium we went to Jordan.

In Jordan we lived in a house we rented for $300 a month. My two sons, 14 and 16, had jobs in a barbershop for tips and in a grocery store for $3 a day. In Jordan we stayed one year. The people that owned the house told us what to do and how to go about getting the papers.

When we went to the United Nations, at the first meeting we were asked all kinds of details, like, "What happened?

"Why are you here?" "What's your story?" "How many children do you have?" "The size of your family?" and all those kind of questions. It was all details.

Four months later we had the second meeting.

The file went from the UN to the Canadian Embassy. We don't know why, but I think it's just luck that we came to Canada, and that we have relatives here.

Then the Canadians asked us many questions as well. I had to repeat the whole thing. It took about 3 or 4 hours. Then we waited one month to find out. Then we found out that my son has a disability, so we waited another month and we got accepted, and then it was another month until we got our visas. The church brought us here to Canada.

When we were in the hall, I got a virus from a man who had pneumonia. If I didn't get over that, we wouldn't have been able to come to Canada.

During that time, though, we were much less worried. We felt that what we experienced before was much worse than what we saw ahead of us.

14. Bernice Dewick– Independence in Wartime

This is just part of my introspection of what makes me the way I am. I think it would be interesting for people to realize what it was like in Canada in British Columbia in North Burnaby, growing up during the War. My experience of doing that is I was born in 1940, right at the beginning of the war. My father was in the war, and my uncle was in the war, and all of their friends. And they were gone. So we were a culture of children raised by women. And we were raised by women collectively. In my case, there were three women: my mother, my aunt, and our neighbour, whose husband was also in the war. And between us, there were six children. We were raised by one of those three mothers while the other two were out working at the shipyard rivetting – that's what my mother did – and other jobs for the war effort. So there was this continual changing of mothers, and six kids were raised as one family.

You know, one of the things that really stood out in my mind, we were raised at a time when there was this overlying sadness, all the time. Because the fathers were gone, the women were overwrought with fear and hard work, and we were always getting information of the loss of their school buddies, of their friends or of family who had died. And that sort of – I never realized it until I got older and had to think about it – but one of the things that it did for me, growing up that way, we were there six years like this, so it's your most formative years, is that I knew I could never ever rely completely on a man. Because the men didn't come home. Then the women had to figure out what they were going to do. I knew I had to have my own skills and be self-sufficient and independent. It was so deeply entrenched in me, not only did I take it to heed for myself, but I also forced it on my three daughters. They were all raised to be independent women, and that was because of the reality that you can't rely on another person to be there, even though they want to be there, they just might not make it back.

15. Eeman – My Brother's Death

Someone knocked on the door at work. My sister and brother-in-law came and told me, "Come with us."

I said, "Where?"

She said, "Mahdi, your brother. They're looking for him."

I went home to our place and there was a lot of upheaval. My brother's three daughters were crying. Yesterday he was killed.

My mother took me to see him. We went to the place where they washed his body. I saw his body and his eyes were open. We were all crying. I kissed him, and he was cold, but he was smiling.

They brought him home and they couldn't bring him into the house. So we sat in the garden. His wife was crying, saying, "I want to see his face." They opened the wrapping, and he looked beautiful. They wouldn't allow his wife to kiss him, but his brother was allowed to. They took him very quickly. Within 10 minutes he was gone.

He was a soldier, and left the army. He was killed by the militia.

I continued to work as a hairdresser, but in 2005 people came and threatened me and beat me up because being a hairdresser was against their beliefs. At 9 o'clock I came home, and they had blown up everything that I ever owned. 6 months later I went to Syria.

At the same time, my cousin was killed, so I left. All this happened in Iraq. It was the civil war. My cousin was kidnapped and tortured. I can't forget. She wasn't even working. She was going to get papers from Iraq to Syria, but her family used to work for Saddam Hussein's government, so they kidnapped her and killed her.

In 2007 I went to Syria. I continued to work as a hairdresser, but then things got worse between the Sunni and the Shia. I was in Halab, Syria. My brother was killed in Iraq in 2009. They found his mobile and called my sister and they said, "You're his sister? We just called to inform you that he has been blown up."

There must have been 50 people blown up, and he was one of them. He was in the army and he came home, and at 6 o'clock, they said, "You have to go back." So he did.

It was an IED. Two cars blown up. His body parts were all messed up. They couldn't put him back together. They couldn't tell which parts belonged to which person.

My sister went back to Iraq, and I was lost. Lost and confused.

In 2007 I was accepted to go to America, but in 2013 I was still waiting to go to the US, but then they transferred my papers to Canada, and I said, "Yes."

Then I had a meeting and they gave a choice. I said, "It doesn't matter." I told them my story; I gave them all the details of how they beat me up and blew up my hairdressing. I had a brother who was killed in the Iran/Iraq war as well, in the 80's.

I have lost so many siblings and my mother is still in Baghdad, very ill. She lost her sight and her legs are bad.

I remember everything as if it was yesterday. My brothers were decent men. They read the Koran. They never hurt anybody.

16. Mona E. – Revolution in Ethiopia

I am the eldest of four children. My parents are Egyptians. My father went to work in Ethiopia. Then he came back to Egypt and got married to my Mum, and came back to Ethiopia, and I was born there. I have a younger sister then two younger brothers.

I finished high school in England, and then I went to university. At first I went to a technical college in London for two years, and then I went to Leeds and I got a degree in Food Science, because my father always wanted us to have a business and start a food manufacturing plant in Ethiopia. So I took my degree in Food Science. But when I went back to Ethiopia 1974 there was a revolution. Hailie Selassie was deposed in 1974, so that was a very, very difficult time for all of us. Our house was confiscated. We were in limbo.

We had dreams. Between 1974 and 1976 my father and I went to Europe, and we looked at machinery for him to buy. In fact we wanted to make Nutella. We wanted to start a factory for Nutella in Ethiopia. So we went to their franchise factory, and they talked about machinery and everything.

Then we went back to Ethiopia, but on our way back my father got pneumonia in Egypt and he passed away. So all those dreams went out the window. That was just the time when they were confiscating our property, and my Dad was kind of heartbroken. All his work went to the government.

In 1976-77 I went back to Ethiopia and helped my mother to take care of our business. We had an import-export business, and while they confiscated our property, they left us with the mortgage and the debt to pay off. My father had transferred the business debt to the mortgage, and we had to pay off the debt before we could leave the country.

We had a duplex, and the government wanted to confiscate half of it. They took everything else, and then they wanted that. So they came to my home and arrested my brother as a hostage until we paid off that money. I forgot how much exactly, but they wanted three years paid retroactive.

It was Good Friday, and it was Easter Weekend my brother was arrested. My Mum managed to pay a down-payment and negotiate, and got him out of jail on Easter Monday, and then they continued to pay off the debt.

My brother, after he was released, he stayed on until about 1986 before we paid off our debts. He wasn't allowed to leave, because he had to get an exit visa. You couldn't get an exit visa unless they looked at all your accounts to find out what you owed. So my mother spent another ten years paying off the mortgage.

Whoever had any property, it was confiscated. Fortunately for us we didn't take Ethiopian nationality. The only thing we had to do was pay our debts, and we could leave any time. The Ethiopians had it more difficult. They weren't allowed to leave.

I stayed a year in Ethiopia, and there was a lot of turmoil. A lot of fear. We used to sleep to the sound of bullets every night. I went to Egypt and worked there a year, and then I emigrated to Canada in 1979.

I found out about the famine when I was at school in England. The famine was the reason Hailie Selassie was overthrown. It was in 1973-74 when the Emperor had a big birthday party and people were starving in the interior, and they were all walking towards the big city towards the capitol city looking for food, and the government built a wall and wouldn't let them come in.

There was a British Journalist named Dingleby. He's the one that exposed it all. I was in England at the time, and I found out.

I heard a story about Haillie Selassie feeding his dogs steak, but I don't know if it's true. Apparently he was afraid of being poisoned, and he fed the dogs to see if the food was being poisoned.

17. Kahil Harji – The Coup

My Mum and their family were living in Africa, but at that time there was a coup, and a coup is a civil war. So one day there were bombing planes and there were tanks everywhere. So they had to go to my uncle's house., It was a much sturdier house, but they had to climb a 5-foot wall to get there. The family climbed the wall, but then they remembered. "Oh, no. My 65-year-old grandma can't climb the wall."

And she was like, "I'm not climbing that wall. There's no way, uh-uh. I'm not climbing the wall" So she said, "bring me a chai, and you guys go."

They said, "Okay." So they quickly ran and got the chai, and put it on the patio, and she sat there.

Someone broke into the house. Everyone was leaning against the wall listening to what my grandma was saying. The people that broke in said, "Give me all your money!" and trying to steal everything in the house. So they searched the house and came to the back. They saw the grandma sitting on the chair. "What are we going to do with the grandma?"

There was no purpose for doing anything with the grandma. She said, "Take what you want and leave. Go. Get out."

They sorta shrugged, and there was nothing in the house because everything had been taken out. So they left.

Then my uncle on the other side of the wall was saying, "Oh, there's a tunnel for food. Why don't we just dig it up. So my grandma can come over

Then my grandpa and my uncle and his brother started digging. They went all the way through to the other side, and then Grandma crawled under and they survived the coup.

18. Jack Donohue – Forbidden Pictures

Thirteen years ago my Mom and Dad went to Iran because my Dad was writing an article about an Iranian airline, and my Mom was a photographer. The airline representative was named Husain. In Iran, the government doesn't want anybody to take pictures of government property, because think you might be a spy.

After Husain had shown my Mom and Dad around the airport hangers, they drove by an area next to the runway where they saw some airplanes lined up next to each other. Husain said that Mum should get out and take a picture, but she was unsure. She asked Husain if it was okay, and he said that it was and that he had clearance. So my Mum got out of the car, still unsure, but she still took some pictures. She got back in the car, and a few seconds later two security police cars came speeding towards them.

Husain said, "Quick, pass me the roll of film."

So my Mum gave him the roll of film and he put it in his sock, and she put a new roll of film in her camera.

The police asked my Mum if she'd taken any pictures, and she said, "Only one," which wasn't true, because she'd taken a few more.

So the police escorted my Mum, Husain and my Dad to the airport police office, where they questioned Husain while Mum and Dad stayed in the car. My Mum was really scared because she didn't want to go to an Iranian jail.

An hour later Husain came out with the camera, but they'd taken out the new roll of film. But they still had the roll in Husain's sock.

19. Bernie Moon – War

My family in Korea, I had six brothers and sisters plus my parents. But now I have lost both my parents and still have five brothers and sisters in Korea. I was born before the Korean War. I was 6 years old when I experienced the Korean War. During the Korean War my house was pretty big so the North Korean Army occupied my house as their office, so I saw the very bad: some torturing people and killing people.

My father was a civil servant but unfortunately my father's younger brother worked for the North Korean side, and at that time it was a very serious crime. So my father's younger brother was killed by the Korean police, and then my father resigned from the civil service and went back to being a farmer, as my grandfather was.

When I grew up I voluntarily attended the Viet Nam War in 1966. Then I moved to Viet Nam and worked there. The Korean Army hurt the Vietnamese people, and the Korean government gave compensation to the victims. At that time my English was better than now, so I was an interpreter along with the Vietnamese interpreter and we had to work together. We had trouble finding the victims. They had either died or moved. I experienced this several times.

But also that was a very dangerous job. When we brought them money, we were ambushed on the way. So that was very dangerous. One of my friends with the same job as mine was ambushed and died. Usually the term of service in Viet Nam was more than one year, but after 10 months I strongly requested to return to Korea, because my friend was dead and my mental state had some problems.

But the sad news is that the children in Vietnam never cried. I don't know why, but in Vietnam at that time even seriously hurt children didn't cry at all. That was very shocking.

20. Zong Quin Zhao – Korean War

Before I was born, the Japanese entered China. Many people were killed. For a long time the Chinese people suffered too much pain. I was born in 1945. At that time the Japanese were driven out of China. At that time North Korea and South Korea had their war. China came and helped North Korea. My father was a major, so he took many young people to go to North Korea to help with this war.

I don't know whether it was right or wrong, but I just remember that many young people died. Somebody said that my father died, too. Nobody knew. So my Mom took my younger sister to my grandfather's farm and went back to her family.

Then my father came back alive! So I grew up with my father's family. At that time people of my generation suffered too much pain, with the Second World War and even the

Korean War, and at that time many people in China were very poor.

1966 the Cultural Revolution happened in China. All the people faced suffering again for about ten years. The children couldn't go to school, the workers couldn't work in factories, the universities had no classes. The people had nothing to do for about ten years. Many people in China knew difficult times.

21. John Dewick – Naval Reserve.

The Royal Canadian Navy, in its wisdom, decided to send us back to St. Catharine's, Ontario for basic training, even though we were all from the west coast. In those days it was quite an adventure because you flew back in old DC6s. It was about a 14-hour trip.

Anyhow, I got there, and I guess I didn't realize what a need for freedom I had. I just seemed to go from one disaster to another. Such as the first thing was you're not allowed above decks without your hat on. Well, that happened.

Then I learned you had to do your own laundry. Well, that was a new thing for me. The beauty of it was that the shirts we wore under our dickies were square-cut round the neck, so you could reverse them, so we could get about four days from them by reversing them and turning them inside out. That was one thing.

But the hours were a killer. The ship was divided into two watches, port and starboard watch. When you were in port one watch had to work the ship, the other watch got to go out on the town,

I hooked up with a fellow from Toronto, and we hitchhiked down to Buffalo wearing our uniforms, and a US Marine picked us up. I don't think that bloody car was on the ground more than 30 seconds the whole trip. He just flew.

We got down there and of course the age for drinking down there was 18 whereas in Canada it was 21, so we had to try that out; we did some partying and we got back and the next day I had to sleep it off. So I found the rope locker in the foredeck – it was a little minesweeper – and I fell asleep in the rope locker on the coils of rope.

Then I hear this bloody commotion going on, and it was inspection time.

So I stick my head up like a gopher between the officers and the crew. "What's going on, guys?"

"You! Come here!"

So they strapped an oxygen tank on me, to swim six times around the ship.

My buddy goes, "Haw, haw."

"You! Go with him!"

Then we had to wash the ship, which entailed going over the side on a plank between two ropes with a bucket and a mop. I thought, "This is stupid!" so I got a fire bucket with a round bottom. Of course I kept losing my bucket.

Then I was detailed to paint the fo'c'sle. To do that, I tipped the can of paint up, put it on the deck, and spread it out. The able seaman, head of our section, saw me doing this, said, "Wipe it all up and do it over again."

Like I say, I was going from one disaster to another. Then my buddy and I decided to go to the CNE. That was my first burlesque show. The next day I had to go home, so I was on the plane at 9 o'clock, and by the time I got into Vancouver, when my Mom and Dad picked me up, they thought I'd been dragged through a knothole.

But that was my first breaking loose.

I wasn't really cut out for the discipline of the Navy.

22. Mohammed Rafiq – Escape to Pakistan

The way the decision of the family migration happened was very abrupt. My father was not too much in favour of moving, but one day around midnight we had a bigger town, Sultanpur, near our village, and somebody came to the village from there and said that a massacre was happening, that the Sikhs are killing the Muslims there. The massacre is happening in that town. Those guys, when they finish over there, they are going to come to the village, which was only about two miles from that town.

As soon as that news spread, everybody just left the town and fled into the crops or wherever they could find to hide, because that was going to happen. And that was how the migrations initiated.

I do not remember this. I was four years old. That was what was told to me by my parents and my older brothers. Actually just recently I talked to my eldest brother, and wanted to know the history, and he also charted the road by which we walked all the way to Lahore, which was the border town between Pakistan and India.

Many things happened in that migration. It was the month of August, the hot month. We had to hide ourselves in the crops and then at night travel, then during the day hide somewhere. That is how various people from various places gathered into a big mob. Then everybody found the strength of being together. The whole caravan was walking towards Pakistan.

Various incidents happened in that time. The main thing was that Pakistan did not have much police or forces to protect those people who were coming that way. We were being sort of protected by the forces of the Sikhs and the Hindus. They were not too keen on protecting us. So as the mass was moving we would be surrounded by those people, and they would be looting and trying to find young girls to rape and take away from the mob.

So the people were huddled together to save themselves from that mishap.

In the meantime one truck of Pakistani forces was passing by, and they noticed what was happening, so they did not go further on. They said, "We are going to protect you. What you do is you have the old people and the women and girls in the centre of the mob, and the young people stay on the outside so you can protect them. First, we will protect the whole group."

They were only few in number.

"And then when we get killed, the young people will be there to take over the job."

It was one very delicate day or two days when this was a very delicate thing happening. And then there was a shoot-out between the Indian forces that were supposedly helping and the Pakistani forces that were protecting us, and I think in that shoot-out the Indians left and went away.

So that is how the whole group moved slowly, slowly, to cross the border of Pakistan in Lahore, where they were kept in a refugee camp.

I have just a few glimpses of those times. One was we were standing in the family along a railway line, and there were sugar cane crops growing on the side, and a whole group of people with drawn swords came towards us, and I remember that glimpse, fixed in my mind. When we came to Pakistan my next memories were when I started going to school.

I do not really remember, and I'm glad I do not remember, because those memories would not be pleasant.

My father was an irrigation overseer. When we were at the camp, people were applying to find a job. They had set up a system. He was trying to do that when somebody saw him who knew him.

He was an executive engineer. He saw him standing there, and said, "What are you doing?"

"I am applying for a job."

He was posted in Deraghazikhan and he took my father along and got him a job there. He started his professional life there. There was an irrigation system there, and he was given some responsibilities. He was trained in that, so that is how our life there started.

23. Bernice Dewick – The To-Go Pack, Generation 1

Another chapter in what makes us what we are based on experiences. As I was a young mother with three children living in the Coquitlam-Port Moody area, and my husband was working in downtown Vancouver, I had a real concern for the safety of my children and my responsibility. Now this may sound strange, because we lived in Canada, and we lived in B. C. and we weren't at war. But we were very, very aware that it was the time of the conflict between the United States and Russia, and that was the time of the Bay of Pigs. That was the time when the two Kennedy boys were assassinated, and so we weren't feeling all that safe in British Columbia.

So one of the things I did, is I had an escape route if anything should happen in terms of any sort of military action. How to get my children from Port Moody in the Lower Mainland, out into the Fraser Valley, away from the coastline without crossing a bridge.

My three little girls all knew. Cathy was about seven, Linda was about four or three, and April was two. They all knew that we had to get in the car if anything was happening and we would head right out. We couldn't wait for Daddy; we had to just leave.

24. Cathy Sawatsky – the To-Go Pack Generation 2

This was during the time of the Cold War and we were told by the Canadian Military, in which my husband was a Captain at the time, that the Minot North Dakota Air force Base and missile silos would be a direct target if there was an attack. We lived in Moose Jaw, Saskatchewan, which is 40 miles north of Minot.

As a result of that the military did practices on a monthly basis, where the men and women of the military would be called by an alarm, and they would all have to go into a bunker, leaving behind their dependents and loved ones. If you lived on the base, as we did, the MPS would come around once the siren went, and if the husband or wife who was in the military was home, they would be taken out by the MPs and put in the Deuce-and-a-half truck and taken, whether they wanted to go or not.

There was no opportunity for the enlisted or the officers who were working at the time to contact their dependents or their family to tell them to leave. We were told we had about a five-minute window to get out of the PMQ area. Once the siren had gone off, we needed to leave.

So, having two children of my own, I developed a To-Go kit that was basically a survival kit for about a week. We kept it in the car at all times, and we practised loading up into the car. My children were babies at the time. By the time we left Moose Jaw my oldest, Shawntel, was four, which would have put Matthew at three. So from their birth to that age we practised on a regular basis getting in the car and getting off the base within five minutes. We had three designed routes to go, and we had made arrangements that we would go north to my parents' house, and whatever it took that would be the meeting place, and Don, my husband, knew that when the opportunity came, that's where he would find us, or that's where he could start looking for us.

25. Shawntel Hollis – The To-Go Pack Generation 3

Since moving out of my parents' home I have always had a bug-out bag or five. As the story goes, I have always had this urge to ensure I have enough supplies that I can survive for a month without help. My family would always laugh that if I got lost, they wouldn't have to come looking for me for a couple weeks as they knew I would be fine.

This kit was kept in my car and originally contained: enough food for a month, two cooking stoves, axe, candles to last for two months, wool socks, winter gear, winter boots, three blankets, books on how to survive, fire starting equipment, first aid equipment (including a CPR mask) cooking utensils and visual aids for finding me and my vehicle. Now this was just for the car. My house has always contained enough food for 6 months for four people

When I moved to Creston, I learned I am on a fault line, so my bug-out bag increased. I bought a hiker's backpack and added another first aid kit, clothes, dog food and treats, candles (another months' worth) food for approximately 3 months, toothbrush, comb, makeup, coins, and poncho. I could barely lift this bag, but it was ready. It also contained 1 months' worth of water

Then it gets better. When Bill and I moved in together, I refined my original bag to include 4 emergency blankets, took out the makeup, added Tide to Go, three disposable tooth brushes, more first aid stuff, instructions for CPR, sprains and breaks, CPR mask, two ponchos, socks, wool shawl, fire starters, three knives, water tablets, soap, toilet paper, Kleenex and about $200 in cash

I also made up, if have no weight limit, another bag that has quilted blankets, clothes, more tp, and food.

Then there is the box over the dyer which contains, dog food, treats, toy, 2 boxes of Kraft Dinner, rice, peas, quinoa, two giant garbage bags, one pack of dog poop bags, mints, medication, nail files, tweezers.

We also have our camping gear set up to be a bug-out set (if we are driving) containing enough food for another month worth.

We upgraded the truck's bag to include a cast iron frying pan and a life straw.

Bill's hunting pack has now also become one: first aid kit, life straw, dried food.

We also have a to-go pack for all important papers: bank statements, wills, certificates, USB sticks with picture and programs, files, and $2000 in cash.

About three months ago as I was driving home from Cranbrook I was talking to mom about how Bill thinks I am weird to have all these bags ready to go.

She laughed and said, "Do you know where that came from?"

I said, "No, I just thought I was paranoid."

She laughed and told me how when we lived in Moosejaw, the base would do bug-out practices and mom had bags ready for us and she would pack Matt and me up and head out. .

I laughed and said, "Really? That is where this need comes from?"

Mom then asked me "Do you have a route planned?"

I said "Of course, it involves me getting north to Grandma's in Quesnel." She laughed again and told me she always would say when we got into the car, "Okay, now we are driving to Grandma's."

So there it is. I have had this ingrained into me since mom was pregnant with me.

Currently:

Bag: 4 packs Mr. Noodles, seasoning (garlic, salt, sugar, stevia, pepper, basil, oregano, cumin, aniseed, green onions), teas (herbal, black, green) 1 bag of dried peas, beans, quinoa, brown rice, rice noodles, spaghetti noodles, tuna, oysters, two bags of dog food, dried jerky, KD, two rolls of tp, miso soup pack, veg soup pack, candles, three knives, 5 disposable toothbrushes, one regular toothbrush, tooth paste pick, mittens, socks, 4 emergency blankets, $200 cash, Tide to Go, three antibacterial soaps, cotton ball/swabs, nail file, tweezers, scissors, first aid kit, CPR mask, first aid instructions, underwear, matches, flint, water tablets, $10 in coins, rice packs, homemade dried soup mixes, shampoo, conditioner, 2 ponchos, garbage bags, shawl, and pants, heat packs, flashlights and two large enamelware mugs.

I can carry this one.

3. Occupations

1. Cal Whitehead – Postal Service

For many years we lived between Broadway and 10th Avenue. On an alleyway right across the street from us was a small apartment building, five units, and in the basement was an Irishman. This was in the thirties.

He got a letter one day. Now that's not very unusual, but the letter came from his brother in Ireland. It was addressed to "T. Nelony, Canada." That was it.

So the envelope came, and it said, "Not in Montreal, Try Toronto." And from Toronto, "Not in Toronto, Try Vancouver." And he got it!

His brother had a different conception of what Canada was.

At that time the postman came twice a day, a morning delivery and an afternoon delivery. And sometimes my mother would receive a letter, write an answer and the letter would get to the other person that same afternoon. Can that happen now?

2. Jennifer Melville Roberts – Our Father

Our father was Welsh. Our grandfather was very comfortably off. We know that he was involved with a lot of community things, because he was a barrister. Our father ended up being a merchant in the City of London. I think, but I'm not sure, that it's tied up with the Masonic Lodge. But our father may have been started when he came over to Canada, because he had a fur and leather importing business.

It's interesting, because on Pam's birth certificate, Father is listed "of independent means." On my birth certificate, two years later, it has "merchant in the City of London."

Our father died of cancer when I was four years old, so we don't know much about him. Looking at the photographs we had of him, he never looked a well man. But he fought in WW I.

48

He was British, but he was actually in Canada and joined the Canadian Services.

Three of his friends had travelled across Canada, and when the war started, Father and Sandy joined the Vancouver Regiment. Percy got into the Seaforth Highlanders. In England if you went to private schools they often had army cadet clubs attached to the school. They were connected to a regiment, so that's who they joined. Father joined up as an ordinary soldier, but Percy got a commission immediately. He could have only been in his early twenties. But his family was quite well connected.

Father had a letter from Lloyd George, the British Prime Minister, that his parents had known him in Wales. It's all noted in our father's army record. I don't know how the letter appeared, whether he wrote to Lloyd George to ask for it.

The colonel wrote a letter "recommended for officer by Lloyd George." So he got to be an officer. Then he was seconded to the Royal Air Force. But that's when the Royal Air Force started. He was something to do with the balloons, but we're not sure what, because they didn't say.

So I wonder if his health wasn't great because of the war. It doesn't say anything, but if we looked at our father's pictures, to me he never looked well, but maybe he always looked like that. We don't know.

3. Luz Lopezdee – Pancho Villa

My name is Luz and I am going to tell this story to my grandchildren so that they will have a glimpse of their roots. We are from the Philippines and all of them are born and raised here. So I would like to leave them with the story of their great grandmother who married a guy who became a flyweight world boxing champion in the 1920s.

My mother was 17, and she became widow at the age 19 and had a son that the boxer did not get to meet because the boy was born two days after the death of his dad.

Life has to go on. So my mother became a widow at the age of 19 and met and married my father, of which I am one of the eight children. I would like my grandchildren to hear this because right now the Philippines is enjoying the status of having Mani Pakeou as the boxing champion and so I would like my grandchildren to develop an interest and love for or appreciation for boxing, which is a good Filipino sport. I also would like my grandchildren to remember that they need to know their great grandparents, so that there will always be a connection to where they come from.

I actually have a little email from my daughter who was brought by my mother to a local fight in the Philippines, because she would always be given a chance to give the award, the belt, to the winner of the boxing match.

My mother also had two movies. Two movies were done in the name of Pancho Villa. So there was a Pancho Villa story that was made into a movie and my mother and my half-brother got a little money out of that. So she enjoyed this story of her ex-husband.

When my mother was seventeen, she met a guy from the Visayas, you know, the south. My mother is from a Spanish Family. Concepcion is her name, so they are kind of like the Spanish are: smooth, you know.

Okay, so here comes a guy from the provinces, whether he is boxer or not because he was not yet big then. So her family did not like him because he came from the poor side. He was a bootlegger or whatever, his father left him and so it was not okay. So my grandfather, Julian did not like him.

So the guy according to that was broken-hearted and left and went back to the provinces. That's why they had to elope. Before he left for New York, he told my mother, "I'm going there, I'm going to fight and I'm going to make money. So if you love me..." So they eloped. Okay they eloped, and he left my mom pregnant; that's why he had a son.

So that's how it was, sad as it was. That's part of her journey. She fell in love with a guy who became rich but died soon.

So he was there, in New York, and she was left here. Mother is a Catholic. We came from that part of Manila, Quiapo, which is famous for the Black Nazarene. The story was that in that

50

Quiapo church before a fight she would be there, Sirine, – it was her pet name – Sirine would go on her knees, would walk on her knees as a devotion to the Black Nazerene to ask for Pancho's victory, and it would happen.

Finally he asked her to go to New York. That's why she had a picture in a boat with a hat and all of that and so my uncle would say, "Oh! She would go to the States." And that was a short-lived good life.

But Pancho had a wisdom tooth that was not growing properly and the dentist had to try to open it to pull it out. They were saying to stop the fight but he said, "No, no, no, I'd like it to go on because people are here and they would like to see the fight so it's not fair to stop it or give them back the money."

So he went on with the fight. The fight was not good because he was in pain and he had that swelling so he lost on points. But because it was an overweight fight, the crown was not at stake. He lost the fight, but did not lose the crown before he died. Two days after, the swelling was still there. So they had to deal with the swelling and may be there was already the infection spreading. So they had to bring him to the hospital. The doctor gave him two doses of ether and he said, "Even before the ether took, he died on that table."

But there's another version of the story, which had something to do with fixing fights. But whether it was fixed or whether it was a natural thing, he died two days after the fight. That was July 14, 1925.

So that's it. My uncle would tell me the story of when they brought home his casket. He had to be brought back to Manila because he was a world flyweight champion, the best as far as it's been concerned. When his casket was brought down from the ship there was a siren sounded in Manila to say, "The champion has come home."

For my father and my uncle that was big. I have a picture of my mother facing the casket with her veil, my uncle there and he was such a little guy that my father would say, "That's little

Pancho," because boxing became then a great deal in sports for the Filipinos when he was winning.

So that was the end of his life, and he was buried in the North Cemetery where the ex-Presidents are, and somebody said there's a guy who cleans his monument every day. He probably cleans it every day because he must think that this guy put the Philippines in history.

4. Jack Lillico - My First Magic Show

It was at the Castle Hotel, which was approximately Georgia and Granville, beside the old Birk's building. I was doing a trick that required a big bottle of wine, and I got somebody to come up out of the audience and I poured them a drink, and I poured myself a drink. We enjoyed this drink, and then I cracked the bottle and there was a rat in there. And the problem was that I had painted the inside of the bottle with watercolour and the white rat came out absolutely black. It was a very embarrassing situation.

But I was so nervous that I threw up after the show. The wine didn't help. It was crummy old wine off the shelf at home. Aged.

What you do is you file a bottle around. You make a circle around it and file or saw with a coping saw, and then you wrap a wire around and attach it to an electric coil, and then it cracks, so the label was holding it together with the rat in there and two shots of wine in a test tube attached to the neck of the bottle.

That was my first show when I was about fifteen years old. I had my first book of magic, which I bought in Woolworths for about 20 cents or something, and this book I gave to a guy a couple of years ago. It had the cover torn off, and the back torn off, and it was pretty bad shape, so he got me another one by the computer, an actual print from the 1930 edition, and most of the tricks I used were out of that magazine.

So I've got the old book and the new book, and it's a new old book.

You had to work shows for drunks, and shows geared for kids, and church crowds and various things.

I have about 60 tricks that I would do on the stage.

I still have some tricks, I have linking rings, you know? And a P&0 wand, which is a wand you can do many tricks with. It's a gimmicked wand.

5. Joanne Harris – Working for Room and Board.

When I lived in Montreal one of the girls I was living with got married, and her mother had a place about 50 miles from Montreal, and she went to live in her country home. Well, with this change I decided to work for my board and room for long enough to earn the price of a new fur coat.

What I was expected to do was look after their two little boys when they went out. I did the babysitting, I did their ironing after work, and I washed the dishes. Those were my primary responsibilities. I had every other Sunday off. That was my time. Sometimes I didn't do anything with that time. But that went on for a year, and I bought my fur coat. It was a sheared raccoon coat, which I thought was very elegant. I brought it with me to Vancouver, and I never had occasion to wear it, because the climate was so different.

The mother of one of my neighbours came to visit her from Red Deer, and I said to this lady, "Do you think somebody in Red Deer could use a sheared raccoon coat?"

She said, "Well, I'll take it with me, and see what happens."

Well she shot back when she arrived in Red Deer, and she said she wasn't out of her car for five minutes before she sold my fur coat for $75. And I paid $350 for it. So they got a bargain.

6. Graham Mallett – Teaching Job in Canada

After I left Australia, I was living in London, teaching in a grammar school. I had a really nice job, but it was difficult to make ends meet. London was a very expensive place to live, I found, and I heard that there were teaching jobs in Canada. Now, at that time there was an agreement among a lot of

53

countries in the world, mainly Commonwealth countries, but there were a few others such as US and I think France was involved, where as a teacher you could go and teach for two years in one of the other countries tax free. So I decided I wanted to come to Canada.

I contacted MacDonald House, and they told me that there was somebody coming from British Columbia to interview teachers the next week, and someone from Quebec the week after. Because BC was first, I signed up for an interview. At that time in England they would give you a day off if you were teaching school to apply for another job or to go for an interview, so I went in for the interview

The superintendent, a Mr. Todd from Prince George, was the interviewing person. I had a briefcase full of references and teaching reports and that kind of thing. So I went in and he said, "What do you do?"

I said, "I'm a Biology teacher."

So he pulled out a map of BC and he pointed to about 4 or 5 different places and said, "We have jobs for Biology teachers here, here, here, and here."

I said, "I'd like the job in Mission," because it was close to Vancouver.

So he said, "We have verbal contracts. You're on contract, now. I'll just have it ratified. I'll phone the School Board and make sure they're okay with it."

I said, "Don't you want to see any references?"

He says, "Oh, no. Are you any good?"

I said, "Well, I think I'm very good."

He said, "Well, that's okay, then." They were very short of teachers, as you might gather. All the commonwealth countries were competing with each other for teachers. So there were Canadian teachers going to Australia, and Australian teachers coming here, British teachers going anywhere, and so on.

It was a very interesting thing. I lived in Mission and taught Biology there. I met my wife, Leda, there, and we're still together.

7. Bernadette Law – A Career in Canada.

When I was brought up in China, my mother decided that all the children had to go through high school, and English school, so that they could make a living. So my sisters all graduated. They worked for a few years to help the family, and one by one they got married and moved out.

I did work for a few years, helping the family, but I wanted to go to Canada to study Art. I told my mother that it was for my career and for my future, so I had to go. My mother didn't think that I would stay long in Canada. So I went there and I studied for four years, and got a job with the Edmonton Art Gallery.

But one day my sister phoned and said that Father was dying, so I had to rush back to Hong Kong. I was with my father for a few days, and he passed away. My mother was very upset, and she didn't want to be alone. She hadn't been by herself, because all my sisters and brother were married. She wanted me to stay with her. I felt pity for my mother, and I got a job in Hong Kong. But I had to go back to Canada to get my things packed up and return to Hong Kong.

When I got back to Canada my friend told me that if I stayed in Canada for two years then I could get my Canadian citizenship, and I would be free to go back and forth from Hong Kong to Canada. So that was a good idea. At the same time, the director of the Edmonton Art Gallery called me and said that the renovation was almost finished, and we can move into the new Art Gallery, and there were so many things that I liked to do, and I could do them in the new Art Gallery.

I thought, "That's great, you know. I can get my dream fulfilled. In Canada I have my future, my dream, and my career. I have to be selfish for myself, you know, once in a while."

So I phoned my mother, and I said, "Just give me two years, and I'll be back with you."

She was in Hong Kong. She couldn't drag me back from Canada. So she said to herself, "I can't depend on my children for joy and happiness. I should be independent. I need to have help. So she began to get up at five o'clock in the morning and walked up to the top of the mountain and did her exercises with fresh air. She did that every day, rain or shine. When she got back from her exercises she came home for breakfast, and then went to the seniors' centre just across the street. She took some programs to keep herself busy.

After two years, when I got my citizenship, I went back to see my mother. In the morning, she'd say, "Oh, I have to go up the mountain and do my exercises, but I will come home for breakfast."

After breakfast, she'd say, "I have to go across the street to the seniors' centre, I have my Hawaiian dance this morning."

She came back for lunch, and she'd say, "Oh, I have my Tai Chi class in the afternoon." She did this almost every day. She'd say, "Why don't you go look up your old classmates and go shopping with them?"

I came home on purpose to keep her company, but she didn't have time for me. So I just wondered how she really did at that time, and my niece told me that she was very interested in Drama, and she wrote scripts, and directed, and also performed, and made costumes for all the performers, and she enjoyed performing Hawaiian dances in different places where the group was called. She really had a chance to find out what she liked in life, and she didn't know that she had that much talent. She only had Grade 6 education in China, but she was doing very well.

So I'd been feeling bad for two years, leaving my mother, and being selfish, and doing my own things in Canada, but I found out that it wasn't a bad decision, because my mother had a chance to find herself and develop her talents. She was doing this and enjoying her life.

When she was 80 years old she had an operation, and the night before the operation the nurse asked her to take a sleeping pill, and she didn't take it. And the next morning they couldn't find her, but at 7 o'clock, there she was, saying, "Here I am for the operation."

They said, "Where have you been?"

She said, "You know, after the operation I have to stay without exercise, so before the operation, I had to do my exercises." People thought that she was afraid of the operation, and sneaked away, but she was living by herself and all independent and enjoying herself.

I still have brothers and sisters in Hong Kong. They are only one call away; you know Hong Kong is such a small place. She was fine looking after herself and happy. In her 90th year, one day she was not feeling well, and they asked her to go to the hospital that night, but she said, "Oh, no, I don't want to go."

The next morning she couldn't get up, and they took her to the hospital, and she died within 24 hours. That is the way she always thought. "I don't want to bother people. I want to be happy as long as I can be independent, I can live as long as I want. But if I can't do anything, there's no point of surviving in that kind of condition. She really had a good life, and I admire my mother, and actually I do a lot of the things she was doing.

4. Logging

Editor's Note. Horses are more intelligent than you might think. It was common practice in horse logging for the men working in the bush to hook a log on behind the horse and send it down the skid road by itself. The horse would pull the log to the landing, where the mill hands would unhook the log, turn the horse loose on the skid road, and send it back to the bush, all on its own.

1. Tom Brown – Horse Logging

We moved down to Carwells road, and my uncle started a sawmill there, and that would be I guess probably when I was about 7 years old. They started logging there with the sawmill. At that time they logged with horses. They would bring the timber in to the mill. My Dad and my uncle started this sawmill close to where we lived, and at that time there was no machinery around, so they had to hire hand fallers to go out with crosscut saws and fall the trees, and cut them to length with the saw, and they had a team of horses they'd hook them onto the logs and haul them into the mill.

Then when they got too far out from the mill for the horses to pull all that way they made a skid road with a sled, and they put notches for the log to run in, and then you put some grease on them, and they went out nearly a mile, I guess. The bush team, they would fall the logs into the landing, and load it onto the sled, and the horses would pull it in.

That's what I used to like doing. I was going to school then, and boy, I'd run home, and they'd put me up on the horses, because they liked to get the horse to go by himself, but they'd put me up and I could drive the horse down and back.

We were out probably a mile or more, and at quitting time they'd just put the hames up and turn the horse loose, and I'd sit up there and I'd ride the horse home.

They logged for a while like that, but then the Depression hit, so they couldn't sell the logs, they just folded it up. I don't think anyone could buy anything, then.

It was a small operation. I think they only had about four or five horses.

They used an arch, there, too. It had big, high wheels. The axle went in and it was bent up, and they had arms on it. When they pulled it, it would stand up straight, and the bent axle would come down to the log, and they'd put a strap on the log.

Then they had blocks on the wheels, and a rope or cable from the long tongue up there, and the horses would pull and lift the front of the logs a foot off the ground, and then the horses could pull a lot of logs.

They tried lots of things. I remember my uncle got one of the first tractors. It had no blade on it, and it would get stuck, and if you stopped that thing it would dig a hole so deep it wouldn't come out because it had big cleats on the wheels. They'd have to tow it out with the horses.

The tractor had a skid pan behind it. They'd roll logs on that, but the problem with that was, again, it didn't work back in those days. It was all trial by error.

They had a pretty good sawmill because they had a steam engine running it. I was too young to notice much.

2. Tom Brown – Sawdust Selling

I went to town, my brother and I, and started a sawdust business. My uncle had a truck business, and he left, and my oldest brother, Walter said, "Arnie's gone up to Alice Arm to work and we can take over his business." We had this old car there, and he asked me to bring it to town and he could get this truck. I lived in this apartment. I got the neighbour to come and hook on with his mother's car, I guess, and we put a tire between them and towed my car to town.

So we were in the sawdust business, selling sawdust and wood. We had a contract to buy it down at Eburn sawmills, and you could go in a hopper there and fill sacks up and take it out to the people, and they all had sawdust burners on their stoves. It was tough, because we had to pack them down into the basements.

They trimmed wood, I guess wood was cheap then, because they had trimmings and slabs, so we'd buy them at different lengths, and we had a sawmill and we cut them into stovewood and sell them. It was a lot of work for not much money.

3. Tom Brown – By Wagon to Hope

My Dad always found some sort of work, even though he had no education, and I think he couldn't read or write.

Just before the War, Dad got a job up at Hope on the Hope-Princeton Highway. He was logging in there with a shingle sawmill at that time, hauling shingle bolts out of the bush. He phoned me. I guess when I was selling sawdust.

A fella was hauling shingle bolts in with a horse and wagon, and the road got so steep that the wagon was running away and he was having trouble with that. Dad got the bright idea to get an old truck with mechanical brakes on it and tear everything off and put a tongue on the front for the horses, and a lever for the brakes, and so we made that.

That was my first job. He had a team of horses down here that he wanted to use for hauling shingle bolts. So he loaded me up on the wagon with some hay and stuff, and I drove from Langley. The first day I went down through Langley here, up to Vedder Crossing. There was this big barn, and I stayed there the first night. The next night I went up to Hope, where Dad knew the Reed Brothers. They owned the car dealership, and I stayed there overnight. The next night I went up to the camp just below the slide.

I think it's 75 miles. Because it's 100 miles from Vancouver to Hope. 2 and a half days. I was making twenty-five miles a day, because to Vedder Crossing from here must be...I'm not sure. I should know because at that time they used to have a mile post every mile, and I got to counting them going by.

Then I hauled shingle bolts back. The wagon with the brakes worked well.

I worked there until I went in the army.

4. Tom Brown – After the War

After the war I came back and then right away I started logging up here in Langley. I started a little sawmill up on 204th and up at Willoughby and worked there. My partner was my now-brother-in-law, Ab, my friend who married my wife's sister.

Not long after coming home from the War, June and I got married. We went to Vancouver Island for our honeymoon, and then I was back to working at the sawmill. We lived in a little old schoolhouse made into a sort of house. We were very poor, and June was very good at making do. Of course, we were raised with nothing, so it hadn't changed. Dad was still pulling logs for us from the areas around. All the brothers were helping.

We did that for about a year, and then we saw an ad in the paper for a sawmill to come to Saturna Island. Ab and I decided we should go, so we just told the wives to pack up and we loaded everything on a barge and we got on the CPR boat that serviced all the coast, then.

Soon we were living there. There were nice families there, and while we worked hard, we made good friends, too.

At that time Alan came with me with the family. They had a school there at Saturna. We were at Boot Bay, and the school was down at the end of Lyle Harbour, so they could walk; it was a couple of miles.

The one fella he built a kayak, closed in with two seats on it, and he and Alan paddled that to school.

We sawed lumber for one year, and cut about 200,000 board feet, I guess. So we got this scow, and we loaded it up to ship to Victoria, and on the way over I guess it was a little our fault, the guy was new there, and he had a boat, and it wasn't probably big enough and he was towing across there and a storm came up and dumped the whole scow of lumber in the salt chuck.

We picked up a fair amount of it. Lucky it was fairly close in, and there were logging people there we knew, and they had a bunch of boom sticks and they had two boats, and they grabbed that and went out in a big sweep and they corralled a lot of it and they brought it in. It was heart-breaking, and we didn't make much money.

So then after that's when I went into logging, because at that time we were out of money, and the kids and the family were starving to death, so I started logging with the Pohl Brothers, an outfit that I got to know. While we were there, they moved in and started logging there.

I needed money then, so I started working for them, and worked for a year or two, and it was good, because I got some experience with them. With them I could do everything; I got to run the Caterpillar, drive truck, monkey wrench. It kept me interested, and that has been a hard thing to do all my life.

We logged for about two years on Saturna Island, and we ran out of timber. So the boys I was logging with moved up the Theodosia Arm. There was no school for Al and the other kids there, and I decided I didn't want to do that. On Saturna there was a store and a government wharf, with fuel pumps and a boat stop for fishermen and tug boats and the fella was getting old, and he talked me into buying it. So I bought the store and the wharf on Saturna, and I ran it for a while, but I didn't like that job. That wasn't for me. I was a logger. That store business is completely different. Lucky my wife, June put up with running it for the year. She had our daughter to look after, too, so when another opportunity came up she was glad to leave. Little did she know what she was getting into next!

But the Pohl boys had finished at Theodosia Arm and went up to Jervis Inlet, and they were really hollering at me to come to work for them, come to work for them, and I didn't like the store. It was hard to get supplies, hard to get the locals to pay their bills, and no one was ever satisfied, no matter how hard you tried. It was remote Island living and it was hard all the way around.

So I was lucky. I sold it and we packed up and went to Jervis and started working up there with them. Saturna island was remote, but it was paradise, compared to Crabapple Creek Logging Company.

They had just bought this timber and on the front they'd logged a mile back with a-frames, and they yarded the logs down to the water. But now it was too far to yard, and we had to truck it. Which meant we needed a road. We had to start from scratch, build a camp and start building road to a mile up the hill where the new timber was.

When we went to Saturna we'd only been married a little while. We were living in Langley, and I said to my wife, "Come on, pack up, we'll go to Saturna. And we went to different places around Saturna.

"Pack up and move here, pack up and move there."

Then, in 1950, it was, "Pack up, we'll go up to Jervis."

"What's it like up there?"

I said, "I don't know, but the boys are up there, and they've told me it's all right, so I guess it is."

So we packed up, but then we had to come back down to the CPR dock in Vancouver. The boat left there at 9 in the morning and got up to camp about 10:30 at night. When we got up there, the boys hadn't done anything, just piled the buildings wherever they could, just had a float anchored out in deep enough water. They had just dumped the camp and all the equipment there on the shore and hadn't set up anything. When the boat from Vancouver dropped us off, there were some other people there.

One guy said to my wife, "Come on, I'll take you ashore."

And it was dark, of course, and she got in the rowboat, and this fellow rowed in and stopped, and he said, "It's time to get out."

And she got out, up to her knees in water, and she had our three-year-old daughter, Sherry and the dog and the cat in her arms, and she said, "Where do I go?"

He said, "Oh, there's a house up there."

So she goes up there, and it's just a bunkhouse, and it's sitting at an angle, and there's no lights or anything. She had to crawl into it without any help because I was waiting to get all our stuff off the boat.

Anyways, she wasn't too happy.

We were pretty close to Princess Louisa Inlet, and the boat dropped us off and went up there and tied up overnight, and came back down to Vancouver in the morning.

And my wife told me later, "Boy, I was sure thinking if there was some way to get out there, I would have flagged that boat down and went back to town!"

And you could. You just put up a flag and the boat would pick you up and take you to Vancouver. But she didn't know that.

But she was amazing, and the next day, I took the bulldozer and moved the buildings around, hooked up gravity water lines out of the creek and set up a lighting plant for a little power. It was a terrible time, but we survived. The freighter was our lifeline, but you had to be organized. Each week you ordered what you needed and it would come next week. Nothing in between. Hard lessons to learn.

5. Tom Brown – Runaway

When we first got the Letourneau skidder, we were going up a really steep hill. Al used to lay in the back and sleep there going up the hill, because the fuel tank was there, and it was flat.

I heard a big bang and I looked down and the air gauge was gone. There were no check valves in the lines, and it blew off right at the compressor. That machine had air clutches in it. It steered just like a Cat. You had to release a steering clutch and step on the brake, a skid steerer. Those clutches both were air, and the transmission was air, and the brakes were air. Once you lost your air, it was free-wheeling. I yelled, "Jump" and he was like a bullet, he was out of there. It had an electric blade, and I wanted to get the blade down because it was so steep that it didn't go over backwards, we had a piece of D8 blade and filled the blade with water to keep the front end down. So I thought if I could get the blade down, but it's electric, and the machine was backing down faster and faster.

I was worried about Al, because there wasn't much room. The bank was steep, and it went right over. I figured, you know, maybe he'd get hit. But he sneaked by it.

It was going too fast for me, so I jumped out, too. So it backed down, and the arch went over the bank, and there was a log there, and the tire hit the log, and the arch went back out on the road and it headed down again. And we thought, "Boy! It's gonna make it!"

But then it went over right by the edge, and we thought, "There it goes." But there was another rock there; it bounced off of that, turned around and nosed into the bank. Broke a wheel off, but there it was. We coulda stayed right on it and it wouldn'ta hurt us.

Right away then I put a check valve everywhere, so that if that had happened then, everything else would have had its air, and I could have stopped. But we were in such a hurry to get logging, because they'd been out of it so long, and we were just so happy, it gets that time, I didn't even think of it. That reminded me pretty quick.

And that's what was so good about Al up in camp; no matter what it was he would do it with me. Lots of times there was a road, when we were hauling like that. With dragging you can't have ditches because they wear wood off and bark, and when it starts to rain, it rains so heavy that it'll wash, and when it comes to a cross ditch, the stuff will stop there and the water will go over it, and once it goes by one, it'll just build up, and it'll go right down a road and wash the darn thing out there, because sometimes it rains for two or three days or a week.

So sometimes if it started to rain, even in the middle of the night, I'd just call Al, and we'd go up and clean out the ditches. And the creek going through camp, it would get so high there would be big boulders, we could hear them rolling down there like thunder. One night it got so high it took our tank out. We had a light plant, and I thought it was going too, so I was out there, and Al was holding the rope, and my brother Howard, and I was hooking it up, and they were supposed to pull me out if I fell. They were like that. Al could do everything in camp.

Al was our blasting guy. It was very dangerous for him because no matter how much you plan, rocks and trees that have been displaced will go where they want. He was good at his job, though, and I always felt lucky to have my brothers around. For some years I had my oldest brother Walter as well.

In the winter months there was too much snow to work so we would come to town and stay with June's folks in Langley. My Dad would stay in camp and keep things from freezing. It was a lonely time, but he seemed to like it. The only communication was the radiotelephone, which worked only if the weather was good enough.

Thinking back on all this, it's a wonder it all happened.

66

6. Allan Brown – Blasting

I started with Tom building roads. I don't know why, I just kinda liked the work, and the road finished here, and I went from there and hired out with another one of the cats. I went up into Lockbar Inlet with another company, with Orlandi Brothers Company and went working for them. I was about 25 or something like that.

After I finished building road for a while I went down to Port Melon. At that time there was big burning pits down there, and they were doing salvage on the shores right in Port Melon. Then that shut down, too. There was a sawmill there. This company that I was blasting for built a sawmill down there, so I worked there, too.

I kinda stopped blasting then. But I did blast for I guess it was about 20 years I was blasting up there. I must have been about 40 when I moved out of there.

Once at Port Melon, there was one rock there and I don't really know what happened. I probably put too much in it. There was a piece went over the edge. I had my camper on my truck I was living in. And then a rock did go right over and it went right through the roof. It wasn't a big rock, but it was coming pretty fast, and it went right through the roof. So I had to get the camper fixed, I sent it away. But that was really the only bad accident I had. I was lucky. I was careful all the time. You had to be.

We blasted a rock, it was a big one, and we loaded it on the Euclid. Sometimes I would even drive the truck, and this loader guy loaded this big rock on, and I went to go up because there was a steep road and I had to go up to the top and turn around and come down, and that big boulder, we just drill a small hole in them and blast it into pieces. It was pretty hard because you had to blast and we never cleaned the face off or anything, so we had to blast pretty careful to get some breakage.

The drill was a huge diesel powered air drill, and an arm with a jackhammer on it to drill sideways into the face of the rock. And then smaller ones to hold it in place. And then this hammer went along with ten-foot holes, each steel made a ten-foot hole, then you'd add ten-foot steel rods and go in 40 or 50 feet. It was loud and rough and your whole body shook all day long.

Then you set the shots, and wire all the holes all up. To get the breakage you have to be careful. Each cap has a number on it from zero up to ten or twenty, to tell you how slow the timer is. So then you set them so they break and come in together. They start at the inside and then keep workin' out on each side, and then when you blast they come together and break the rock up. The time delay for each one would be about a second.

The caps have two wires on them so you hook each cap all along. It only takes a second, and it all runs down.

Mostly I learned on the job. Bet there were books and instructions. For years it was okay, but then the methods changed and you had to be registered. I had to have a blasting ticket.

It took me a long time. I'd study it up, and I'd go to town for a week, and I'd come back and – no ticket. There's a lot of theory in there. Finally I got my ticket, and that was good, because when my brother Tom closed the camp, I was able to go to work for others.

Stumps, we'd go and put so much powder into them and blow them out of the ground. Now they have different machines that just dig around and pop them up.

We were on the turn skidder, and we were going up the hill and a big boulder came down right in the road. Luckily it wasn't too far from the shed where we stored our water. "Oh, I'll blast it for you."

So I backed the machine down and he went got the powder box, and I was down doing maintenance on the machine, and pretty soon he comes running down. "Get under the machine!"

I said, "Whataya done?"

"Get under!"

And when it went, it just about blew us out of there.

"What are you doing?"

Our dynamite was the same. If you wanted to take a stump out, you used 20%, and it was real slow and it would lift the stump out. If you wanted to blast a rock like that you used 75 or 80%. He just opened up a case and put a cap in it and a fuse. And it did, it split the rock, so I could push it over the edge.

One time at another job a helper took the dynamite out of the wrong box. This guy put a box of 80% on the rock, and threw a cap in it. It was a crazy time but the rock did split. All the leaves came off the trees for a long way around.

Sometimes the rigging bringing in the logs would loosen big rocks, and they would come tumbling down the hill going in any direction. Sometimes logs would get loose on the turn of the rigging or they would catch on another log. You had to have eyes in the back of your head.

One time we were loading up a load at the landing. If a rock came the whistle punk would blow a warning whistle. This day a whistle went, and I could see everyone running and ducking. I got out of the machine, and this great big rock came rolling and it was coming right at the machine. I guess I froze, not knowing what to do, but lucky there was a stump there, and the rock hit the stump and went over and went just behind the arch with a turn of logs, and it took the turn of logs off the arch with a bang.

7. Gordon Long – B. C. Interior Logging with Art Long

Dad came back from WWII, married Mum and used his Army payout to buy a sawmill and set himself up in business. He logged across Decker Lake from Palling, and up the Thomson Creek Valley, where, coincidentally, he had a trap line. This was useful when the beavers used to make dams and flood out the logging road, because he could legally trap them and sell their furs, finding a silver lining in that cloud.

Here are a few stories my brother Sandy and I remember of the early 1950s, growing up in a small logging camp.

Our father learned his logging growing up on a homestead farm in Palling, B. C., just about the centre of the province between Prince George and Prince Rupert. His father, Jack

69

Long, had moved up there in the mid-1920s when Dad was about 7 years old. Through the Depression, they farmed in the summer and logged in the winter, mostly hacking railroad ties for the Canadian National Railway.

Our father worked through the transition from old-time to modern logging. He started out cutting down trees with a cross-cut saw, hacking them into ties with a broad axe and taking them to the railway on a horse-drawn sleigh or wagon. Sawmills were set up in the bush, and the horses dragged the logs from the stump to the mill, one at a time.

By the end of his career they were cutting the trees with feller-bunchers, pulling logs to the road with diesel-powered skidders and hauling them in trucks to mills closer to town and the railway.

The only thing that hasn't changed that much is the trucks. If you Google Image "Logging truck 1950," you'll see a dual-wheeled truck with rotating bunks with tall stakes on them, and a trailer with the same rig. The trailer gets hoisted on the back of the truck when going back to the bush empty. A modern logging truck will have two or even three driving axles, and up to three on the trailer as well, but it's recognizable as the same machine.

The lumber trucks are similar. Dad's "Dear John," a 1952 Ford, had six wheels on two axles and a flat wooden deck that would carry the equivalent of two lifts of lumber. The modern Super B-Trains have flat wooden decks, but two trailers and up to 38 wheels on as many as 9 axles, and they carry about 36 lifts. But still the same idea.

The interesting difference is loading and unloading the lumber trucks. Nowadays it's all done by forklifts, so it's boring. In the old days, they had no machines for handling the lumber, so they had to use their ingenuity.

The boards were carried out of the sawmill and piled by hand in stacks the width of a truck deck. One end rested on the mill floor, which was raised the height of a truck off the ground, and the other end rested on a portable wooden frame just the height of a truck deck.

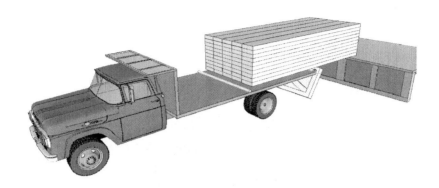

The back end of the deck on the truck had a metal roller stretching the full width, and they had a portable roller that could be placed on the empty deck. When it came time to load, the truck would back under the lumber, and the solid roller would lift the load enough that the frame could be removed. Then the truck would continue to back in, finally lifting the other end of the load off the mill deck. Binder chains would attach the load to the truck, and away the truck would go.

The fun part came at the planer yard, getting the lumber off the truck. The binder chains would be changed, so that they only went around the load and were not attached to the truck. Then the truck would back up rapidly and slam on the brakes. The load, sitting on rollers, would scoot off the back of the truck and crash to the ground.

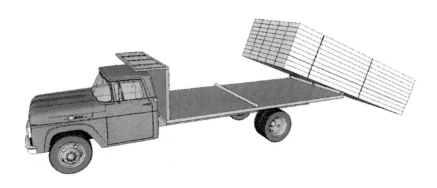

It got really fun when the lumber was over-long, because then as the lumber rolled backward it would reach a point, just before the load tipped off, where the weight of the load behind the axle would be heavier than the front of the truck. This meant the cab of the truck would rise until the tail of the load touched the ground, over two metres in the air. Then the driver would pull forward, and the cab would come crashing down.

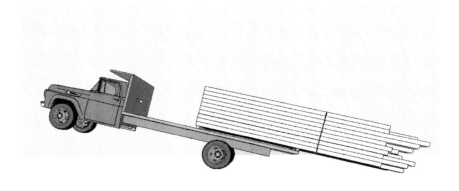

As kids, we always loved watching that.

Needless to say, with treatment like this and narrow, rough, logging roads, these trucks got pretty trashed. At the end of their careers they were no longer safe to drive on the highway, so they were converted for off-road logging. What was left of the fenders was taken off to increase visibility. Doors were removed to allow the driver a quick exit in case of a runaway, which happened frequently, as they were often operating with no brakes.

But Dad 's work came full circle. In the '70s, everybody was going back to the old ways, back to the land. Dad left logging and went building custom log homes. He was a founding member of the British Columbia Log House Builders' Association. He actually taught Log House Building and Horse

Logging at College of New Caledonia in Prince George and at Yukon College in Whitehorse.

8. Gordon Long – Art Long, Later Life

Dad was self-educated. He left school at Grade 8 because there was no further schooling available. He learned from reading and travelling. His mother had been a terror for proper speech, so he could speak good English if he chose to.

But he loved to play the hick and then surprise people. For example, in his early sixties he and Mum took a trip around the Greek islands on a cruise ship. One activity provided was shooting skeet off the afterdeck. Dad watched for a while, and then asked, "Can I try?"

"Have you ever shot skeet before?"

"Nope."

So the guy hands Dad a shotgun, and Dad stands there, waiting. Most people put the gun to their shoulder and stand in shooting position. Not Dad. He just held the gun waist-high.

The guy says, "Are you ready?"

Dad says, "Yep. Let 'er rip."

So the guy shrugs his shoulders and pops the throwing arm.

Dad whips the gun up to his shoulder and blasts the clay pigeon out of the air. Then he does the same thing five more times.

Of course, Dad had been hunting duck with a shotgun, and moose and deer with a rifle, since he was a kid. He had passed his sniper's qualifications during the War. But, in truth, he had never shot skeet before. He just liked to have fun with people.

His standard out-for-the-evening wear was a tweed sports jacket with suede elbow patches. So he's dressed like that at dinner on the cruise, and this lady looks at him and says, "I wonder what you do for a living? I bet you're a college professor."

Dad has that twinkle in his eye. "That's right, I am."

"I knew it! What do you teach?"

"Log House Building and Horse Logging."

He always got a chuckle out of that story.

5. Daily Lives

1. Nathanial Headley – Skateboard

My story is set last summer, two days before school started. I had my friend over, and we played some video games and had a lot of fun, because it was summer, right? So a little bit later it was time for him to go home. I asked my Mum if I could ride with him half way to his house.

My Mum said, "Yes," and I was so excited, because it was the first time she had ever let me go out on my skateboard by myself. But as the garage door went up, we saw that it was raining. Not hard, but a light rain.

So I put on all my protective gear and I grabbed my skateboard and rode with him halfway to his house. When we got halfway to his house, I said, "Good-bye. I'll see you in two days."

As I was riding back, I'd just like to point out that it was a rainy day, and my board got really slippery. I hit a big rock, and I went all the way over into a pile of rocks. As I was falling, I put my left arm out and I landed on it.

As I got up, I looked at both my arms. My right seemed fine, but my left arm seemed a little bent, and it hurt. I got up and ran all the way to my house. My Mum was watching me from the balcony, so she knew I was in pain. She ran down, got me into the car and we sped straight to the hospital.

I had to go through an exam, and my arm was broken in two places. So I got my cast and went home.

As we got home I remembered that I left my skate board out there, but it was gone. Somebody stole it. That's my story.

2. Cal Whitehead – The Depression

I was born in Canada, in Vancouver. My parents had come down from the Rocky Mountain area of Cranbrook and married in 1923 and they had four children – my mother's plan – very quickly. The last one was born in 1928, just in time for the Depression.

When the Depression started the bank they had their money in went belly up. So here they were with four preschool children right at the beginning of the Depression. So we moved across the city to what is now Prince Albert Street. It was Burns Street then, near the streetcar line so my father could get to work and back.

I had two younger brothers and one of the stories I have in this small house we changed the dining room into a bedroom for my sister and my brothers and me. At first my brother Frank and I shared a bed. It was toward my fifth birthday, in cold weather, and I woke up one night and I felt wet in the bed.

And I shouted, "Mum, Frankie wet the bed again."

And my Mother came in. She said, "Shield your eyes, I'm going to turn on the light." So she did. She pulled back the covers and there was our mother cat. She had given birth to four little kittens and was licking away at them and not paying any attention to us.

But she was between my brother Frank and me.

Mum had that funny look on her face when she saw any baby; she just had a look. And then she replaced the covers very carefully and said, "We've disturbed her enough. Roll over and go back to sleep." Which I did.

But I considered those kittens mine. They were Mine!

That's the sort of thing that went on.

I eventually did go to Grade 1 and Grade 2, etcetera, and I ended up with a university degree.

My parents were both avid supporters of education, although he only went to Grade 4, and she left Grade 9 in order to get married at the age of 15.

When they saw me graduating, getting my degree, there was that look on their faces that was the same as when they saw a baby.

3. Nathan Kwok – Skiing

I'm driving up to Whistler, and we're going to have a good time at Whistler. We're going for the weekend. So we get up there, we ski for like the entire time, and then we go to this one run. Oh, boy. That run was hilarious. The chair lift to get to the run was terrifying. It was terrifying. We go on the chair, and the person in front of us clips his ski on the bar and falls on his face. And then he tries to roll over to the side.

I tried to go over to get on the next chair, because I didn't see him. And my Mum's pulling me back. I get clipped by the chair, and I'm pulling on my Mum to pull me back, but instead of that I push on her, and she's sprawling across the snow.

Then she's rolling around and I'm on the chair going up by myself. I'm terrified, because it's pretty high up from the ground, and if I fall...I'm dead.

My Mum's just sprawled across the snow, and my family's friends are picking her up, and we're going up. And then I get off and I ski down, and I had a fun day after that.

4. Mohammed Rafiq – Getting Used to Canada.

When I came to Canada, although I had a brother, and I had an education in English, I had a problem with the accent of the people. The speed with which they spoke English made it difficult for me to grasp what they were saying. Also the street language, the slang, was different, because some of the words they used were not found in the dictionary, and I didn't know what they meant. Those were the two main things that I found difficult. I tried to stay around people from Pakistan or people whose English I could comfortably understand, but I had to get adjusted here.

I gradually started watching TV and hearing how the people spoke the language and what kind of accent was used. Getting used to the society here was very important.

When I came to Vancouver, there was a New Citizens' Reception Centre, which was a small office downtown on Granville Street. I got introduced to that, and I found that a very useful way to communicate with the community and understand the system here and the various education sources and all that. That is where I started learning English.

There were no classes. They just gave us references.

But one thing that they did, they had a newcomers' dance every month, where various people came. I didn't know how to dance, even Pakistani dances, not to talk of Canadian dancing. But I found it very interesting to talk and meet people from different countries. That, I found was a very good thing.

Then, a year later, my wife joined me,

I got married in Pakistan, and I was here at university for the first year, because I did not want any distractions from my studies. It was going to be hard studies, changing into a new education system. Also, as a graduate student, I was supposed to have an "A" in every subject, or I would be kicked out of the university. The first year was a qualifying year, which mean that you study at your own expense, and you have to get an "A" in every subject.

So I took that challenge, and thank God I passed it.

For that my brother gave me a few hundred dollars, and I got a student loan from the university. I lived at Dog Patch in Fort Camp Residence, where I was given a small cubicle with only one bed and a small table, and if you got out of bed, your second step would be out in the corridor. I found it difficult to cope when I got up in the morning over there, and everybody had a towel on their shoulders and nothing else, going to take a shower.

That is how I started out here.

But thank God I took that challenge and I passed it and I was passed on to the PhD program. I had such good marks that everybody was amazed. Some of it was my presence of mind, which gave me good marks, but some of it was hard work, hard studying.

5. Trace Johnston – Missing Money.

This was quite a few years ago at my grandma's house; we were there for Easter dinner. My grandma had taken money out of the bank but she misplaced it, and she had no idea where she put it. It was quite a few hours before dinner was going to start, and she told us how she misplaced it so we looked all around the house. We couldn't find it. We looked literally everywhere. We even looked in the kitty litter, because she had done the kitty litter that day. We really wanted to find it so we looked everywhere. We even looked in the garbage.

And finally we were just going to have dinner, and just before we sat down she looked in her bra for some reason, and it was in there. We all started laughing, and now whenever we have a family dinner we tell this story.

6. Karan Gill – Sewer Jumping

My story starts in India where my family and I go for the holidays. We were at a party at my aunt's house. It was a pretty boring party, so my cousin and I decided that we were going out back to take a walk and just talk. He was 14 and I was 7.

We were walking along this sewer kind of thing. He was just joking around and decided to see if I would jump across the sewer. He thought he could stop me before I actually did it, but he couldn't.

I jumped, and unfortunately it was too big, and I ended up right in the middle of it. So I got the mud all over my pants. My cousin helped me up but he got really mad.

"Why did you jump there? I was joking!"

I was, like, "You were the one who told me to jump!" I mean, really. I said, "I'm sorry, when you say, 'Jump,' I assume you mean, 'Jump'!"

I thought things couldn't get any worse, but they got worse. All of a sudden, I hear barking. I turn around and see this huge black dog barking at me. I just panicked. I thought, "I'm going to die. I'm too young to die!" And then I realized the dog was on the other side of the sewer, so he couldn't get to me.

But I ran as fast as I could all the way to the house. I saw the door. I was almost there, and then I hear the barking again. I turn around and the dog was standing there again. It chased us, and we ran to the door.

I opened the door. I jumped through, and then I remembered that I had the mud – at least that's what I called it; I don't want to think what it really was – all over my pants. Now it was all over the carpet.

As you can probably guess, I got in a lot of trouble. But one good thing was, my cousin got in more trouble.

7. Elaine Vaughan – Can You Believe It?

This is the story of an ex-boyfriend of mine years and years ago back in university. We went up to my parents' cabin one summer, up in Vernon, on Kalamalka Lake. We were going to go waterskiing behind the boat, but Dave was a little bit hesitant.

I'm like, "Come on, Dave. You're a real active person. Why wouldn't you want to go waterskiing?"

And he said, "Well, let me tell you."

A few years back Dave had been out on the water, on a floating dock quite far from shore. People would hang out and maybe someone would come by with a boat and take them for a ride and then drop them off at the float again.

He was on this floating dock with a friend of his and his brother, sunbathing. Some other people were out on the water towing behind boats.

All of a sudden, his brother turns around and Dave isn't there. The brother's like, "Dave? Where did he go?"

I mean, they're sunbathing, and all of a sudden he's gone.

Well, unbeknownst to everybody, what had happened was that a boat had gone by, and the skier was done skiing so he let the rope go. And the end of the rope lassoed Dave, right around his neck. Dave was lying there, sunbathing, and this rope came flying through the air and went around his neck and yanked him off the dock.

Thankfully, I guess the driver of the boat sensed that there was a drag. This all happened so quickly. Dave's brother noticed that Dave was gone, and then the boat driver turned around and they figured out what happened and went in and got him. He was unconscious, but they were able to get him out of the water before he drowned.

It blew my mind. You know, you think certain things would never happen? Well, that's one of those things that could never happen, and I actually know the guy it happened to. And he's a great guy and has had a great life ever since. But he isn't a great fan of waterskiing.

8. Ishan Kumar – Monkeyshines

This story takes place in Asia. I was walking on a high mountain, at a high elevation. I was walking to this village, and on the side of the walkway there were long poles, and on the top of the poles there was a tarp.

And on the tarp there were monkeys pushing each other off the edge. You could see monkeys flying off.

We were going for a walk and my parents went ahead a bit. At this time I was only three. I was looking at the monkeys and a monkey came behind me and pulled down my pants. I fell on the ground, and there were people all around me looking at me. They lifted me up, and then my parents came back.

Then that monkey ran away, and we didn't really see where he went. He didn't get my pants. I still had my pants, and I put them back on and then I went into a store and a guy gave me a lollypop. And that's the story of how the monkey pulled down my pants.

9. Ken Donohue – Eggs = Huevos

We used to live in a townhouse complex, and one night I was doing some baking and we didn't have any eggs. So I thought I'd just go to our next-door neighbours and get some eggs from them and everything would be fine. Our next-door neighbours were originally from Peru and they spoke Spanish and English.

So I went across and knocked on the door. The Grandma answered. She was visiting from Peru, and she didn't speak

English. I don't speak Spanish, and I didn't know the word for 'egg' in Spanish. What was I going to do?

I decided to act out an egg. So I gestured, "I need an egg."

And she just looked at me blankly, like, "What is this guy doing?"

I tried to show an egg, and then I pretended to crack an egg. And she just stared at me and she had no idea what I was saying.

So I thought, "Okay, I'll pretend I'm a chicken." So there I was at her door, flapping around, and she still had no idea what I wanted, so I gave up. I just gave up and went home.

The next day I was on the bus, and her son, who is about my age, was on the bus as well, and he said, "My mother said you came by."

And I said, "Oh, yes, I was looking for an egg."

And he said, "She thought you wanted a chicken."

And I now know that "huevo" is the Spanish word for "egg."

10. Jas Kooner – Speaking English

This happened a long time ago when I was very little, and I didn't know any English. But I didn't know that I didn't know any English. That's what kids think when they're little. They think they actually understand everything when really they don't.

I must have been about three at that time, and my Mum was taking some English lessons because she didn't understand English either, and she wanted to be with it and she wanted to be able to have a job and do all kinds of things here in Canada. So she would take English lessons at the public library, which was where her tutor was. This was in Vancouver, at the library on Fraserview.

So she would go there, and she had to take me along because she didn't have childcare. While we were there, they had a story time, and I loved books, even though I couldn't read. I loved books then, and I love books now.

At that time I noticed that all the kids were sitting there and listening to a story. There was somebody sitting there holding the book and reading the book, so I'm thinking, "I can go there and listen, too."

Except before they could sit down to listen, they were going up to this other woman, and they were all lining up. The woman was saying something to them, they were responding, she was writing something and then she was hanging it over their necks. As an adult and as a teacher, I now realize that it was a name tag.

I got in the line and waited my turn. I got all the way up to the front, and she said something to me. It probably sounded like, you know, when you listen to the adults in Charlie Brown TV shows, "Wa-wa-wa-wa-wa." That's what I heard.

And I was so proud that she was speaking English to me, and I was going to speak English back, darn it, even if I only knew one word. I only knew one word in English, and it was "Safeway." So she said, probably, "What is your name?"

And I said, "Safeway."

And she's like, "No, wa-wa-wa-wa."

And I was pretty angry. I'm like, "I know my English." So I said, "Safeway," again.

And again, she's like, "No, I'm not writing this down," and she wouldn't write it down, and she sent me to the back of the line.

And I stomped off, and I was kinda like, "I want to listen to the story. How dare she not write 'Safeway' down for me?"

So I just waited and waited, and there was some kid who ripped off her nametag and it was lying on the ground. So I just took the nametag, and I put it around my neck, and darn it, I went and heard that story!

And now, every September in my class we always do nametags, and everybody writes their name on, and everybody sticks them on their desks.

And every time, I feel like putting down, "Safeway."

11. Georgia van de Bon and Addison Shaw – Playland

Georgia:

Addi and I and my parents decided to go to Playland one day in the summer. We started driving the car, and it took a long time to get to Playland.

Finally, when we got there we had to drive around the whole entire parking lot to find a spot. And we ended up a long ways away from the parking lot, and our car ran out of gas. So my Dad had to go get gas and put it in the car, and we had to wait for another parking spot.

Finally, after about 45 minutes or an hour, we found a parking spot, and we had gas. We got out of the car and we got into Playland.

Addi:

The first thing we did is we wanted to ride this big ride called the Beast. We were really excited. So we got on the ride, and it was terrible. We both threw up after. It was disgusting. Then we got lunch. For lunch we had hotdogs and a drink, and we had popcorn

Georgia:

Then we went to the haunted house. For the haunted house we got in there, and it was so scary. We went through it and people were popping out of everywhere, and they were supposed to not be able to touch you or grab you, but there was a person grabbing your ankle. Addi and I both tripped and fell. She banged her head and I hit my whole knee and it was all bruised up and swollen and I got a hole in my leggings.

After the Haunted House we went on the Ferris wheel. We were having fun except someone had thrown up on the Ferris wheel before us, and they barely cleaned it up, and it smelled disgusting, and there was still a little puddle of it, and it was just disgusting.

After we got on the Ferris wheel we were at the very top and the ride stopped in the middle and it took about half an hour to get the ride working again, and we were freaking out because it was swinging back and forth and it was just really scary.

Addi:

After the Haunted House we were pretty much done with Playland and we just wanted to go home. But a few weeks later we went to Playland again and it was much more fun. I guess we just had bad luck that day.

12. Joanne Harris – Knitting

Now, about 12 years ago I knitted what I thought was a beautiful poncho in brown mohair with rust stripes. It took me a couple of weeks, and when it came off the needles, I put it on and decided to go to the mall to flaunt it. And I told myself, "I'm going to keep walking until somebody notices this poncho."

So I'm walking and I'm walking and I'm walking, and I'm getting hungry and I'm getting thirsty. These people are blind! They haven't noticed my poncho.

Finally a lady passed me, and she backed up, and she said, "Hey that's a beautiful poncho you're wearing."

I said, "Oh, thank you. Now I can go home."

So the next day I went to Kin Village for lunch, wearing my poncho. And the first person that saw me said, "That's a beautiful poncho you're wearing."

And I impulsively said, "Oh, would you like to buy it?"

And she said, "Yes."

And I thought, "Oh, dear. What'll I charge her?" I spent $30 on the wool, and I thought, "I'd better charge her $35. A steal."

But then this lady asked me if we ever go to Point Roberts for lunches.

I said, "No."

And she went on about the community centre there, and what a good chef they have, and so with that my husband and I started going to point Roberts for lunch every Wednesday and Friday, and we've done this ever since, for eleven or twelve years. So that's what developed from having worn my poncho.

13. Elija P. White – Thomas the Train Tantrum

My Dad was gonna take me to Toy Traders so we could play with the wooden toy Thomas Trains, and then we'd go back and have some lunch, and that'd be okay.

So I was playing with the trains and having fun, because I loved trains back them. It was like a half an hour later when my Dad smelled something really, really, odd. He smelt it, and he knew right away what it was. I pooped my pants.

So he's like, "Oh, no, we've got to get Eli out of here."

So he slowly walks up to me and whispers in my ear, "Come on, Eli. We've gotta go."

I'm like, "No! I wanta stay!"

He's like, "No, we have to go."

And then I'm like, "NO, I DON'T WANT TO GO!" So I'm screaming and crying, and he tries to pick me up and grab me out of there, and everybody's just staring at us like "Okay…"

But before he could grab me I grabbed one of the toy trains and I whipped it at his head.

Now he's just ticked off. My Dad's just ticked off. He's, "Okay, I'm done. I'm done."

So, he just grabs me and then he storms out of the Toy Traders, and he brings me in the car and he's like, "Okay, we're having lunch now. We're gone!"

14. Mik Roberts – Movies

A couple of months ago my family and I went to watch The Great Wall in the Guildford Movie Theatre, and we had a lot of trouble there.

It started off pretty good. We were at a really good part in the movie. But then, out of the blue, a couple behind us started talking uncontrollably. We shushed them a couple of times, and they never stopped. They stared at us, and then we exchanged looks. Once we did that, they actually stopped talking.

Right as soon as I thought that everything was going to be perfectly fine and we were going to be able to finish watching the movie, a little girl (in a PG-13 movie) started crying and whining in the seat to the right of us. The father had taken the baby out a couple of times. But as soon as the father would take the baby out it would get quiet for a second, and then the couple would start talking again.

So for the entire movie it was an on-again-off-again thing the entire time. There never was a long period of time when we were actually watching the movie without any distractions. But then right at the end, when everything was over, when we got out, the baby wasn't crying and you couldn't hear the couple talking.

6. A Full Life

1. Kartar Singh Meet – Family Life in India

I'm Kartar Singh Meet. I was born in India in 1941. My father was born around the 1890s. There was a famine in India. My grandparents had sold their land; rather I'll say they mortgaged their land to other people. There were 3 brothers in my father's family. They had to eat the rotten wheat issued by the government to the people. My father, whenever he narrated his childhood, told me, "Even when I think of those days, I can still feel the stench and taste in my stomach and mouth." It was utter poverty in the last decade of the 19th century when my father was born.

My father enlisted in the British Indian Army in 1909 at the age of 16 or 17. He fought in World War I and fought in Burma as well as in the Middle East. He was a Regimental Sergeant-Major. In those times, there was only one such person to be a Non-Commissioned Officer of about eight to nine hundred people. It used to be a big honor in those days. When my father retired after about 23 years of service, he was 40+.

I had 2 uncles. Though they had been able to retrieve their land from the people they mortgaged it to, they were not able to get married, because females were less in number and they had passed their marriageable age. Boys especially, and even the girls, once they reached 25 they were considered as having passed. Generally the girls were advised to get married around 18, 19 or 20. Even I got married when I was nineteen and a half.

So my father's cousin's wife taunted my father. My uncle had bought a woman. In those days, females could be bought from other parts of the country. My uncle bought a woman for 700 rupees. They produced no child and therefore my aunt told my father and uncles if they died, their properties and the retrieved one would go to her sons. My dad was 42 and he took it as a challenge. He said, "It's a matter of honor." And he married.

My maternal grandmother was a widow with 3 daughters and no son. My father had to pay a considerable amount to get married to my mother, because at 40+ he had no chance to marry a woman. So my mom was around 15 or 16 and dad was 42 and they produced 11 children. Eight of them survived. He was 78 when he died in '68. When my youngest brother was born, the 11th one in succession over a period of 28 years, my father was 70 years old. He was fertile. Because he had devoted all his life time to service in the military, honestly. He was very intelligent, so he had devoted his later time to more religious study.

When I got married, my youngest brother was 7 months old and my mom felt ashamed, because in our society it's considered a taboo for the women to have young children when their older children get married. And my youngest brother, by the way, is younger than his own nephews. My sisters were married in '53 and this boy was born on 20th December '59. So his nephews and nieces were 6 or 7 years older than him. And then when I got married, my mom used to feel embarrassed because my wife was there. That means if my father or mother didn't take precautions I would have had another brother and he and my daughter would be playing together. It's something funny in our society. That is one unforgettable memory.

2. Dorothea Lowndes – My Father

My Dad was a military man, very strict, very demanding and very scary sometimes. I had ten brothers and sisters. My mom came from an Italian background, and we lived close to the army barracks. We had an interesting life. We didn't have too much because ten kids are hard to support, so I don't remember having any shoes that were brand new. They came from my older sister to me and so on. But we still had a great life. I was number two in the family.

I missed a lot of stuff. I started going to school. I loved politics at that time. I used to get involved in anything that meant politics. And I was real outspoken. And sometimes I got into trouble.

Especially with my father. "Don't you answer me!"

I respect my family a lot. Especially my Dad, even though he could be a bugger sometimes. Not very fair. But I knew he had a heck of a job trying to educate ten kids and being there for all of us. Now I know and appreciate it even more.

He used to tell us stories. He loved weapons, because he was a military man, in high rank. And I remember he had almost an arsenal in the bedroom. Nobody, none of the boys, could go in the bedroom and touch anything. I was too nosy, and I always wanted to see how they worked.

I don't know if he did this to teach me a lesson. He came home one day with a German machine gun. He said, "You want to see this one?"

I was about twelve. I said, "Not really, you know." A big thing like that.

He said, "Let's go in the back yard." We had a big back yard.

And he said, "Put it against your shoulder, and when I tell you, 'Press the trigger,' you press it."

The wall there was bricks, about a metre high, and I said, "I really don't want to do this."

And he said, "Well, you're going to do it. You're going to do it. I'm not asking you. You're going to do it."

And I was shaking, you know. I was worried about dropping and breaking it. That would get me in trouble. Nothing else.

But I put it against my shoulder like he said, pointed, and when I pulled the trigger it hit me in the shoulder.

He said, "Pay attention to what you are doing. Don't be a chicken."

I said, "I don't want to learn this. I'm not going to need this, ever."

He said, "I'm not asking you, just do it."

Well, what happened was we had holes in the wall all over the place, and that was my experience with the German machine gun And I think the name of that machine gun, they called it Ludinha . Never forgot that name.

It was a very interesting life, growing up in a family like that. We lived in places that were not so nice. I remember he made a place to keep chickens because Mom liked chickens.

And of course we kids didn't have much place to play and there was a wall about a meter high, and we used to play around and run around, and one day I jumped inside to see what was happening there and my Dad was coming from the army for lunch, and he said to me, "Don't move."

I said, "why?"

He said, "Don't move." There was a coral snake. Right underneath my feet, and I hadn't seen it. So I froze. He said, "Don't move; just stay where you are."

And he took his gun and shot the thing, and me there, saying, "Don't make a mistake."

It was very frightening, but I think it gave me a tremendous amount of, I wouldn't say courage, but open eyes. You can't panic. Don't cry. That was one thing. "Stop crying. Don't be so silly. Don't be soft. Don't cry."

It took me a long time to be able to open up and say, "I'm scared. I'm scared."

"No, you're not scared. It's no good to be scared, I'm telling you."

"Well, OK."

So in that sense in my future life it helped me a lot to be the way he taught me, because I had to survive in some different places, so I was grateful for that. Very grateful.

3. Dorothea Lowndes – Marrying an Englishman

I met my husband in Brazil, in our little city outside Sao Paolo. I didn't speak English, and he didn't speak Portuguese, so it was interesting for us. My English was what I was learning in school. Verbs and all that. At the time I was 19 years old, and he was 24.

I was going to a Catholic school, a private school. It was an incredible effort my father had to make when he had 5 kids to pay for school at that time.

I understood more than I could speak. By the time I got out a sentence, we were talking about something else.

So that's how we started.

He was very, very polite, very nice, very handsome, too. That was my weak point, because he was tall and I was short, and all the girls around that little city were after him. I said, "What did he see in me?"

For the next few weeks we used to meet in a garden; there was a small place you could walk around, you know, an old-fashioned city, and people talked about everything, and people talked about us.

I said, "I've got to talk to my Dad before he finds out."

My Dad was a military man and very strict, very, very strict.

I had to face my Dad and ask him, and tell him I'm marrying a man, I'm 19 years old, but I want to go back to England with him.

And my Dad just looked at me and says, "You're not serious. You're crazy."

And my fiancée wasn't there, and he said "what kind of man is this comes to Brazil and just…"

I said to him "You know, we're in love."

"What do you mean you're in love? You just met him, you know."

He said, "You don't even know this guy. You're going back to England, and he's going to leave you there. You can't speak English, you don't know anybody, what are you going to do?

I said, "I'm going to go, with or without your permission."

He said, "I don't want to talk to you any more."

So I wrote him a letter, 'cause I didn't have the courage to tell him everything. So this fellow told my Mom, and my mom was a saint, and I wrote everything. I said, "I want your permission. I want your blessing. But if I can't get it, I'm going to go. Any way I can."

And I wrote everything. I said, "I do hope you accept that I know what I'm doing and I think he knows what he's doing."

And I left the letter for him and went to bed.

I got up in the morning to go to school. I hoped to hear something from him. So he comes in the kitchen, and I'm sitting there, and he looked at me. "You're going to be late for school."

I said, "I'm not going to school."

"What did you say?"

"I'm not going to school."

He said, "Your last year."

I said, "I don't care."

So he stood up and walked away. He didn't talk to me for three days: he wouldn't look at me. If I walked in the room, he walked out.

"Oh," I thought, "How can I go?" I had no money to travel, and I had no clothes to take with me. Because, ten kids, we had a limit. I had my uniform. I couldn't go in my uniform, you know, and what am I going to do?

My future husband said, "How am I going to talk to your Dad? Does he speak English?"

I said, "No. But you're going to be able to tell by his face how upset he's going to be."

But he somehow got up the guts to talk to my Dad, so we went home, and I said, "There's an Englishman that wants to talk to you."

He said, "About what?"

I said, "We are in love and he's going back to England, and he wants me to go with him."

He said, "What?"

I said, "We want to go back together."

He said, "Are you crazy? You don't know this man enough."

It was only six months by that time. I said, "No, but I trust him."

He said, "Why would you trust him? Tell him to come and talk to me."

I said to Colin, "I can't do this," because I had 10 brothers and sisters. It was a big family. I couldn't just walk away from that.

Colin finally said, "Let me talk to everybody, then."

I said, "You can't. They don't speak the language." But anyway, he did. He somehow got the sympathy from my Dad, which was a miracle, because my Dad was really hard.

He said, "Okay, if that's what you want, okay. Go."

4. Dorothea Lowndes – He's Married

Yeah, that was a surprise.

He finally said to me. "I'm married."

I said, "Oh, my God, you're married? I can't tell my Dad that, because my Dad will kill me."

And he said, "No, but we never got along, I've been travelling since we got married. She's five years older than I am, and you know, it's not working out. So it's not because of you that I'm getting a divorce. We were getting a divorce already."

He came to me one night, and he said, "My wife is here. In Brazil. And she wants to meet you."

I was afraid. In a sense. I wasn't afraid of anything, let's put it that way. I said, "Sure." What am I going to do, say, "No"?

So she was in the hotel with him. I was in the club. I saw them coming, and I said, "Wow, she looks a lot older than he does." I was 19, she was about 30. My God, you know, she was old as far as I was concerned, and a very bossy type.

She came, and I went to shake hands. In Brazil women don't shake hands. You kiss on the cheeks, you know? But I thought, "I better not do that. Get slapped in the face."

She was talking to him, and she was a little bit aggressive.

He translated what she was saying. "She said, 'If that is what you want, you can have it.' But she said we have to go back to England to get a divorce."

They had just bought a house and everything because she was all about money.

He said, "You can keep it all, I don't want anything. You can keep it all, we can make it."

Anyway, he said, "I'll see you later." They went back to the hotel. I don't know what happened there. He came back, and he was talking to me, and he had his hand covered up.

I said, "What happened to your hand?"

She smoked cigarettes. She had a cigarette, and she put the cigarette out on his hand.

I said, "Bitch!" and I said in Portuguese, "That's horrible!"

And he said, "Don't worry about that. Don't worry. It's done."

Then we just had to figure out how we were going to England. He was an engineer. He was making good money in Brazil, and I had nothing. Nothing, really.

I said, "I don't want you to give me anything, I don't want you to pay for anything." And I knew my Dad hadn't the money to pay.

He said, "No, I'm going to take you back to England with me. That's the only way I'm going to get a divorce, right?"

That's when we had the discussion with my dad, and he gave me some money to buy clothes. He said, "It's cold there."

And I'll never forget this, and my elder sister didn't let me forget it. I didn't have enough shoes, so I stole my sister's shoes. And I made the mistake in England, I took a picture of myself with the shoes, and she said, "You stole my shoes!"

I had no winter clothes. I had nothing.

From Brazil to England; it was February. You can imagine how nice it was.

So we did it. We had to go to Portugal because he was still married. We went in a ship that was the last trip they were making before the winter storms. It was a horrible trip all the way from Brazil to England. It was just a freighter. It was horrible. Very bad.

He said, "They are going to interview you on the ship. So you tell them you have two hundred pounds."

I didn't even know what pounds were. I said, "How much?"

He said, "Two hundred."

I said, "Okay." At that time that was a lot of money. He was making good money because he was an engineer, but I didn't have any money.

They wanted to know how I was going to be supported in England. I said, "I'm going with him because I want to meet his family. We're just friends."

I'm sure they believed that. But for some reason they said, "Okay." So they stamped my passport. They said, "Okay, you go, and you have three months to stay in England."

And then we were in England.

We couldn't go straight to his Mom and Dad. He had to go by himself and tell his parents, "I brought a girl from Brazil. I'm getting a divorce." All this at one time.

I said, "Oh, my God."

So we got room and board in London. It was a horrible place, horrible place. And you had to put coins in the meter for the light to come up.

Well, he went, and from London to Stockport where they lived was quite a ways, you know, a few hours by bus, because we didn't have a car.

And I'm standing there, and all of a sudden the lights went off. I said, "What do I do now?" I was petrified. "I can't speak to anybody."

So I went to the landlady, and I said, "Can you put the light on, and when my husband comes back he'll give you the money?"

She said, "No, that's not how it works. There's a machine there; you put the coin there, and the electricity comes back."

So I could play with that. So I played with it, and it opened! All the money came out. "I'm rich!" I could have gone to jail, I suppose. Now I just put the coin in and I didn't have to do that any more. So I closed it up, but I kept some coins to keep the light going.

And then the money ran out, and the light went off again, and I said, "Now what?" All the money was in the machine, and I didn't want to open it again, because I was scared, now. So I went outside, and I only had a little shirt on, and pyjamas, and

I was standing outside in London, in not a very nice area, and I saw my husband coming.

He said, "Oh, my God, what are you doing outside? You're not supposed to be here. It's bad for you; they'll think you're a prostitute or something."

I said, "A prostitute? I'm here because I'm cold, I'm scared."

"Don't ever do that again."

I said, "All right, but I had no lights, but I know how to get it." I told him how I got into the machine.

He said, "No, you don't do that! You can't do that."

Anyway he went to his parents and his parents said, "Bring the girl here. Bring her."

And I tried to dress properly to impress them. High heels with snow on the ground. Pink shoes, and the coat that I bought, I was freezing cold, and my legs and my feet were purple.

We got to the house. They were not well off. We knocked on the door, and his father was...if I hadn't been in love with my husband I'd have been in love with him, because he was such a wonderful man. He looked at me and said, "Come on, love."

I said, "Love? That's what they call you?" That was new to me.

I walked in, and he gave me a hug, and he pushed me near the fireplace and he made me take my take my shoes off, and my legs were purple and he was rubbing my legs near the fire. I fell in love with him, he was such a nice man.

He didn't want to know anything. He said, "We have to take care of her. She's a kid."

His mother was absolutely shocked. "Are you crazy? You're going to lose everything."

Colin said, "I don't care, Mum. I don't care. We can start over again."

And Granddad (his name was John) said, "Welcome home."

That was the best thing I ever heard.

They tried to give me some clothes, so they gave me two pounds to buy some shoes, which was a lot of money for them, because they were making five pounds a week.

Colin went to see a lawyer and said he wanted a divorce as soon as possible, and the lawyer said, "The best and quickest way is if she gets pregnant. Then they can't deport her from England back to Brazil."

Well, do you think we could get pregnant? Well we tried very hard, and had a lot of fun trying, but nothing.

I was friendly with this retired Italian lady that I lived across from because I could communicate a bit with her, and one day I said, "I feel so bad, I feel sick, it's the food, you know,"

She said, "I'll take you to the doctor."

She took me to the doctor, and it was a very small area where my husband lived, everybody knew everybody, everybody knew her name, so we came home, and she said. "Good,"

I said, "What?"

She said, "You're pregnant,"

I said, "No. How do you know? I'm not?" I said. "I'm not. Look." You know I was very skinny. I said, "No, I'm not pregnant."

She said, "Oh, yeah. You are."

I said, "I'm NOT. I wish I was. I just feel sick, that's all. It's just the English food, it's horrible, and I can't eat it."

Anyway, she went straight to my mother-in-law, and told all the neighbours "She's pregnant, she's going to have a baby."

I said, "Oh, my God, are you sure?"

She said, "Yes, I'm sure."

So I said, no, I wanted to see this doctor because I didn't believe it.

So her husband had a motorcycle. He was a postman, and he used to drive a motorcycle with a side-car.

He said, "I'll take you to the doctor."

I got in the side-car and went there, and he said, "Yes, you are, you're pregnant."

"Oh," I said, "That's terrific." Oh, I was in seventh heaven.

Anyway Colin's father couldn't stop crying, he was so happy. He said, "Now they won't force you back."

So we got married, and I was six months pregnant.

5. Dorothea Lowndes – Life in Nigeria

After our son was born we left England and went to Nigeria. We were about 9 engineers, English engineers, and we stayed in a hotel for a few days, then we went to an area that they called the New Reservation, which was for the most well-off people. I don't remember if we paid rent or not, but we were there, and it was a very big place but isolated, totally isolated. The only neighbours we had were Nigerians, coloured people. Not that I haven't seen coloured people. Brazil's full of blacks, anyway. I grew up with black kids. But it was all black people.

Our neighbour next door was a doctor, she was a doctor, both Nigerians, and I became friends with them, because I was by myself, I had a child 15 months old and I was already pregnant with Michael, and it was nice to have some connection.

They said, "You can't do any work, here. You have to hire a cook, a bus-boy, a nanny and a gardener. And you have to pay for those, obviously." But that was okay because my husband was making good money. They were installing the first television in West Africa and it was going to be open some time that year, so they were rushing, so they worked two days on, two days off, two days on, two days off. It was incredible.

Most of the time when my husband was on, this English fellow lived with us in the same house because there was four or five bedrooms, more for my safety than anything else. He was a big fellow, a big, big, fellow. He could take me to the doctor if I needed it.

And everything was getting a little bit weird. We had the first cook. He was an older man. And he used to take my boy and walk away with him, and that started worrying me, I started saying, "Where are you taking the baby?"

He said, "No, don't worry." He was much older than us. He said, "No, don't worry, I'm just taking him for fresh air."

I said, "No, no, no, I'm coming too."

So he stopped doing that.

This English fellow, his name was Jack, he was very naïve, a single kid and very innocent. Everybody was good.

I was a bit suspicious because I grew up in a suspicious country. I said, "All right, I don't like that."

The way the cook looked at me when I was by myself used to worry me. Especially when there was no other guys in the house. I used to watch TV, and because they didn't wear any shoes, before I knew he was just behind me. I said, "I don't like that, I feel uncomfortable."

And I had this big stick, and I used to put it behind my back when I was watching TV because at least I could knock his head off. I don't know.

He started saying things, you know, "Very soon we're going to be free from the British."

I said, "Yeah, that will be very nice. But it was good that they came here to help you guys to get where you're going to be, now, and you learn a lot."

And he had a very cheeky smile, and he said, "No. We learn a lot? No. They took everything."

So I said, "I can imagine it's difficult, but..."

He said, "You know, I think about this house here, when we get independent, this house is going to be ours."

I said, "Do you?"

"Oh, yes, everything you have here is going to be ours. And you're going to be mine."

And I smiled like, "You don't scare me." I was petrified. I said, "What do you mean, I'm going to be yours?"

He said, "We're going to take everything."

I said, "Oh, Jesus,"

So that got me petrified, so when the guys came home, my husband and Jack, I said, "This is what they're saying to me."

My husband said, "Let's fire him right now."

So we gave him his money, said, "We don't need you anymore. My wife is going to be cooking." Or whatever. "You can go."

And he looked with a smile, saying, "I believe you." He didn't believe, not at all.

Then a younger guy came, and his name was Cyril. He was a short little fellow, but chunky, and very pleasant and very friendly, and I said, "Oh, that makes a difference."

But he was the boss, not me. I was paying everybody else, but they didn't listen to me, they listened to him. If he said, "You do this," they did it. If I tried, they said, "No, he's the boss."

I said, "This is strange. We pay them but he's the boss."

And he never let me go in the kitchen. Every time I'd say, "Let me see what you're cooking," he'd say, "No, no, no, you can't come in here. This is our area."

I was beginning to wonder. I said, "I'm going to have a baby any time. What am I going to do? Which hospital do I go to?" They had a fantastic learning hospital a few miles from where we lived, and because I was close to having a baby, we went there to find out, "What do we do, here?"

And they said, "Sorry, unless your husband's a doctor, you can't come in. If he worked here, you'd have a place to come, but we can't take you as a patient."

Well, now I'm 7 months pregnant, where do I go? I can't travel. I said, "Where do I go?"

He said, "There's a Catholic hospital out in the bush. There's no road. You make a road with your car. That's where you go. The nuns will take you in."

"Okay."

So my husband was very, very uptight about it, nervous and scared, and just before that this new cook Cyril, started coming closer and closer. Always behind me, never face to face. You know you could sense someone was watching you, and he'd be behind the door looking at me. I don't like that, I don't feel comfortable.

I said, "You like to watch TV, come here. Sit down, you can watch TV."

He said, "No, no, no, I'm just making sure everything's okay."

I said, "Okay, thank you."

He was so charming, but I didn't buy that. I may be cynical, but I don't buy that.

I said, "What are we going to do, when the time comes for me to have a baby?" My first child was very difficult, and I needed to go to a hospital.

So my husband said, "When you're ready, we'll go to the Catholic hospital."

Anyway, we got to the hospital. It was an unbelievable trip because there was no road. I said, "I hope I don't start labour now, because I don't know what we'll do."

But when you're young, you know, everything is an adventure. You believe in so many things, and I had a lot from my father, saying, "Don't ever give up, you're stronger than you think you are, and you're not a coward," and all these things. So I was saying, "I'm not a coward. I'll pretend I'm not a coward."

So we go in there, my husband, Jack holding my son, who was 15 months old, and Colin driving.

When we got there two nuns came, and they said, "We've got nowhere to put you. We have one room, no doors, it's for the people that can't afford to pay anything. That's the best we can do for you, and hopefully everything is going to be okay. But don't change your clothes until the last minute. The window is open, there's no drapes, there is nothing, there is no door to close."

My husband is sitting there, holding the baby, and Jack is sitting there, and Jack said, "Oh, it'll be okay, it'll be okay." He was single, he had no idea.

I said, "No, I'll be okay," and I'm sitting in bed.

Anyway, they stayed there, and the sister came and said, "I'm sorry but you have to leave now, you have to go home, because the child shouldn't be here, because there are so many people."

The traffic was ridiculous. So I'm sitting in bed, I don't want to lie down, and this guy comes, a big black guy, looking in the window. And then he walks in and I had my nails painted, and he's looking at them, touching my hand.

Then the sister comes, and I said, "Please can you come and help me?"

And she said something to him and told him to go away. And she brought a young black girl, maybe 13-14 years old to sit in there with me. So she's sitting there with me, and of course she's totally somewhere else, her mind is somewhere else, and she's looking at me too, a white person having a baby, must be fun, must be different.

I kept saying, "I need to go to the bathroom, I need to go to the bathroom."

She said, "Go."

I said, "Where is the bathroom?"

She said, "Outside."

I said, "Well, I have to go." I was still dressed. I got up, and I started walking, and I looked, and the women who had just had a baby were sleeping with their guys on the floor, and I'm jumping over them. And I said, "Where am I going to go to the bathroom?"

I couldn't close any doors; there were no doors to close.

Then I'm starting to be a little bit scared. And I said, "Pretend you're not."

And I came back, and I started having labour pains, and there was nobody around, so what was I going to do now?

So I said to the girl, "Call the nurse, please, call the Sister."

She said, "No."

I said, "Call the Sister, I'm not well."

She said, "It's early yet." She's telling me it's early yet! "You're okay, you don't look sick."

I said, "I need the sister, I'm holding now."

I see the nurse. I said, "Please come in, I'm having a baby."

And she walked in, and it was God's gift, because it was such an incredible delivery, compared to the first one.

And she said, "Thank God, everything's okay."

Then she left, and she said, "She'll help you."

And I was lying down, and there was blood and everything else. I said to the girl, "Can you help me to clean?"

"You can do yourself. Everybody here does herself."

I said, "I need help." And I was petrified. By that time my husband arrived. I said, "Hold the baby. I don't want to leave the baby." I was petrified they were going to take the baby. I said, "I'll stay here, smelling whatever, but I'm not leaving the baby there."

And my husband said, "Oh, my God."

And they brought a bottle of Chianti, and I think I drank half of it. I'd never drunk wine in my life, but I drank a half bottle of Chianti.

I wanted to get out. I said, "What do we do?"

Then the sister came and said, "The best thing you can do is take your wife home. You have to take care of her. I can't keep her here. We don't have enough staff. We can do nothing to help."

So it was a few hours after, I think we were all drunk already, got in the car with the two kids, and my other son, at the time, he had blisters on his back because of the perspiration, and it was getting infected.

So I had the newborn baby and the 15 months old baby, and I said, "Well, God gave me two kids, this one was so easy, it was like, 'Hey, it's there, it's yours.'"

My dad used to call him "Negro blanco boobo." That was "My little black African baby."

It was very interesting.

6. Dorothea Lowndes – Revolution in Nigeria

After I had the baby, and we went home, that's when we started having a vision of what was coming. Animosity, some kind of threats. Very specific threats. Like, "You're going to be mine. Not just the house. You're going to be mine. You car's going to be mine. You really don't have anything here."

That's when the new cook that I was hoping was going to be better, came one day and this is what he said to me.

"I need some more money."

I said, "We just paid you."

He said, "I want the money now."

I said, "I don't have any money."

And it was lunchtime. My husband and Jack always came home for lunch to make sure everything was okay, and they worked till late at night.

He said, "No, I need the money now. I want the money, now."

I said, "Cyril, "I told you, I don't have the money. Wait till Master comes – they called him Master – and he'll give you the money."

So he turned around – and I could tell he was quite sure of himself – and went to the kitchen and the table was set for lunch. He said. "I want the money."

I said, "No."

He came back, and he had the bush knife that they used to cut the grass, you know, those big ones? He said, "You have to give me the money, now!"

I said, "I don't have it!"

He was swinging the knife back and forth.

I said, "Why don't you put the knife down and we can talk. Put the knife on the table and we'll talk."

So he put the knife down, and I grabbed it.

I said, "Now, I've got the knife. What do you want?"

And at that time I could hear my 15-month-old crying. The baby was asleep, thank God. I thought, "What am I going to do?" But I said, "He's not going to go near my kid."

My husband arrived with Jack. The house was all glass. All the way to the floor. With a balcony and an enormous yard.

And when I looked, I could see the whole village, all the black people, coming through the gate. And they had weapons and stuff like that. So Jack was a big fellow, went to close the window. He said, "Let's close the window."

When he went to close the window a guy got a rock and threw it in his face. He was a big fellow. He jumped off the balcony. He jumped outside and went towards the crowd.

I said, "No, Jack, please don't!" because I could see all those guys going to kill him.

And he hit Jack again, and he got him in his eye, and he was bleeding in his eye. And I said, "Now we're going. We're going now."

My husband said, "Oh, my God!"

I said, "Don't go! Don't!"

He said, "I can't leave Jack by himself." He jumped.

I said, "Oh, Jesus Christ."

The older baby was screaming, and I think it always had an extreme impact on his life, because he was so angry sometimes. You could see his hands. He was always like that, with his hands clenched.

I said, "What am I going to do? Don't fight, don't fight, just get Jack back in."

But it was too late. They were fighting. A guy comes from the back to hit Jack on the head because he was a bigger fellow. My husband was a smaller fellow. Tall, but skinny.

He comes to hit Jack on the back. He jumps and pushed a guy out. Well, they came after him. And then I jumped, and I go and hold him by the waist, and said, "Don't fight, don't fight. They're going to kill all of us."

I was screaming, screaming, not a single soul anywhere to help. And I thought, "We're going to get killed here."

Finally my husband said, "Let's get in the car." The car was parked right in front of the door. Jack gets in the car. I get the baby, my husband gets the other baby, and we're sitting there, and this guy, Cyril the cook, he came in front of the car, he said, "Nobody's moving."

So Jack just put his foot on the gas. "I'll kill you," he said. "We're going to move," and he stepped on the gas.

So Cyril jumped, and we took off like nuts, not knowing where we were going. My reaction at the time, I said, "Let's run away," But where do we go? Go to the company.

And the company guy said, "Look, you can't go back."

They had ripped my clothes; I had nothing on top. I had to cover myself with the baby.

Colin's boss said, "We're going to the police station."

We go there, and the only one they wanted to talk to was me. They didn't want to talk to the guys. Cyril the cook was there. Standing there with an incredible smile, to say, "I told you we will win." And everybody's laughing at me because they can see, you know, a white woman half naked.

But that didn't scare me. I said, "This guy did this. He almost tried to kill us."

It sure worked. The police said, "Look at him. He's a small fellow. We can't believe he did that."

So Colin's boss said, "Get in the car. All of you guys, get in the car and keep driving. Just keep driving."

We went to the closest hotel we could get into. The boss said, "Tonight when it's dark, you guys are going to drive to Lagos," which was quite a drive. "Get on the bloody plane and go to England. Don't come back here."

I had no clothes; I had nothing. I couldn't breastfeed Michael, the baby, because there was nothing there, nothing at all, so I had nothing to give him. Sugar and water; that was for Mike. I wrapped him in a towel, got him there and all I remember was driving like crazy. Don't stop, just keep driving, driving, driving.

When we got there my husband left the car running in the airport. Didn't even bother to shut it off. We had nothing with us. Nothing...nothing.

One lady that was four times as big as my Mom gave me a shirt to put on.

Colin said, "Just get on the plane."

And the people were looking at us, like, "Where are you going?"

And my husband said, "We're going to England. Don't even try to move us out."

And I think they thought, "Oh, my God, these people are really in a horrible situation."

We had no tickets, we had nothing at all. Didn't even have Michael registered. Didn't have time to register him.

So they put us on the plane. They had baskets at that time, and you put the baby in the basket. We put Michael there, and by this time you're not thinking clearly, you just want to go home, we wanted to go home, you know.

We arrived in London, and the guy in the customs looked at us and he said, "Go, just go." He knew exactly what was happening. "Just go."

It was a few days later when they had the biggest revolution and everyone had to leave. We left just in time. If we had waited two days with two kids, maybe we wouldn't have been able to leave. But we left. We got to England with nothing at all, nothing at all.

We rented a car in London and my husband drove I don't know how many hours to Stockport where his parents lived, and everybody in the whole neighbourhood was crying. Especially his Dad, he was such a nice man, he couldn't stop crying, seeing the grandchild that managed to survive.

But that Nigerian told me, "We're going to have all this," and they did, they did.

They destroyed all the installations they had done for TV and everything. And I remember just before that the Prime Minister – I didn't know much about politics – I think it was MacMillan, came to Nigeria and we went to see him in a limousine, and to me it was a big deal. I think they were trying already to do something, but it was too late.

That was in 1960. It was a big mess after that. Big mess.

7. Dorothea Lowndes – Working Around the World

That sounds so exciting. It was, actually. It was exciting. I met my husband and from that job I had three boys, one born in Brazil, one born in Africa, one born in England. All the places that I went to I learned something, even the real bad ones, I think I got something out of it. I got my son from Africa. That was the worst place we ever lived. We lost everything we had, and they almost raped me, and my baby was 15 months old.

I brought something back with me, and he is a great kid. I just love my kids.

England was more funny than tragic. I remember going to the store. My English was very basic. This lady was behind the counter. She said to me "I can't stand these bloody foreigners. They come in, they should at least learn English."

I said, "Oh, no, it's my turn next. What am I going to say?" I understood what she was saying. "I'm a bloody foreigner, too."

But I didn't look like a foreigner, I guess, so that's why she was okay with me.

I said, "Oh, I have to learn English, quick." And I did. I did.

My best teacher was my father-in-law. He was very patient. My mother-in-law was a little bit impatient. Mind you, during the war, they had a tough time, so she wasn't as patient as Granddad. She's say, "You'll never learn English, for God's sake."

And I'd say to my husband, "English is a really difficult language. People don't realize how hard it is. You have to put your tongue between your teeth. Well, that's not normal for me." I couldn't do that.

It was so difficult to make yourself understood sometimes, but because I was like everybody else, white skin, they treated me like I was English. And I pretended I understood. I went home with the wrong stuff many times. I wanted ham; I took bacon, and I don't like bacon. I hated bacon at that time. Things like that.

But it was a great experience for me, England

Brazil was where my last son was born. So I went from Brazil to England and stayed there for two years, from England to Nigeria, Africa, and then they had the revolution and we had to get out. I arrived in London with a 17 months old child and a newborn.

I was too young. I was 23 years old. Two kids, I had to learn English, I had to come to a country, "What kind of food are we eating? I don't even know." I didn't like the English food, to be honest with you. I got used to it; now I like it.

Then Africa. What are we eating? There was this fantastic dish I learned to make, I still make at home. *Kichirain* they call it. It's a mixture of rice and all kinds of meat and vegetables all mixed up and it was quite nice.

The guy that was cook, never showed me how to, so I had to sneak in there and say, "I'm just looking for stuff."

"You don't come in the kitchen."

Not allowed to go in. It's your bloody place, but you're not allowed to go in the kitchen.

It was a good way to learn. I was maybe, not immature, I think I was very mature for my age, because I had two kids already. I stayed by myself most of the time with my kids, with a big stick behind my back. No guns there. I wish I had my Dad's machine gun, but we didn't have any. So it was just a big stick.

I had my third kid there. That was Peter, my dead boy, that was born in Brazil.

We stayed in England almost a year, then we went back to Brazil again. My Dad wrote me a cable that time. He said, "Tell Colin I got a job for him in Brazil. You guys come back right now." Well, there was no job. He was worried sick about me and the kids.

So we got home, a small house with a whole bunch of people, and I bring three extra ones. It was quite interesting.

So we stayed there for a while, and then my husband went to work in Montreal. I couldn't go, I stayed. He came back, and then we decide that the best place was Brazil. The cost of living was cheaper then. Food was plenty. So, if nothing else, we could eat like pigs. We didn't have much, you know, cars and all that, but food? You drop a tomato, and you get a tomato plant in a few weeks growing there. So it was good. My kids loved to stay in Brazil because they had a family.

We came to stay in Canada in 1969. We went to Costa Rica in 1981, and to Dominican Republic later, but we always came back to Canada. All that moving was complicated, but it was a lot of fun for me. It was all a big adventure.

Recently I said, "I think I should go back to Brazil. I think I should go back and stay there for a while."

My eldest son, now 57 years old, said. "You don't want to go there. It's horrible; it's people all over the place trying to rob you, it's full of gangsters and rapes..." and he went on and on and on.

And I let him talk, then I said, "You know what? I have some notes you wrote when we came to Canada."

He said, "You do?"

I said, "Yeah. I'll show you."

And that's my trick. I get everything I write and I keep it.

And his notes said, "Why did we come to this awful place? I don't understand anybody. Nobody wants to speak to me because they don't understand me. They don't want to speak Portuguese. I hate this place. We're poor here. We don't even have a maid."

And he didn't know if that was what he said.

I said, "Yeah, you did. You forget the good times you had in Brazil when you were there. 'Canada, England, no way. I want to stay here.' That's what you said."

It's a good lesson. Everywhere we go we get something good, something bad, and we learn something.

Participants in Book 2

For the safety of relatives and friends still living in their former countries, some of our storytellers have requested that their names be abbreviated or omitted.

1. Badayeva Family: Alex, Olena, Yuliya

The Badayeva family emigrated from Ukraine in 2003. Alex is a businessman. Olena (p. 22) works in Olympic Dairy, and Yuliya is finishing a BSc program at UBC.

2. Allan Brown

I was born in 1932 in Willoughby, the next to youngest in a family of 10 children (two of them died very young). I was brought up in the logging business. I spent 20 years as a blaster, and I still have all my body parts! I retired to Sechelt, and now live across the hall from my brother in Langley Lodge. (p. 4, 67)

3. Tom Brown

I was born in 1923 up in Willoughby, which is close to here, and I lived there until I was three years old, when we moved down to on 200th at the foot of the hill. In total we had 8 children in our family, four girls and four boys. I grew up when Dad was logging with horses, and I loved being out in the woods with the horses. I spent my life logging, building logging roads, and working on logging equipment. I was married for 69 years and raised 2 children. (p. 1, 8, 19, 58, 60, 60, 61, 65)

4. Brenda Casey

I was born in Winnipeg. My father came over after the Russian Revolution to Canada. My mother was born in Canada. I grew up in the north end of Winnipeg, which at the time was a very unique location in Canada in terms of ethnicity and variety and the style of life that people were making. It was the first middle class area that was formally designated as such.

I grew up with other children of immigrant families. Often both parents were immigrants although there were certainly enough people in the neighbourhood who were Canadian born and bred. It was an interesting mixture: different ethnicities and backgrounds. (p. 29)

5. *Darryl Catton*

I was born in Huntsville Ontario, and I lived there until I joined the Air Force when I was 17. I went to school there. I learned my trade in the Air Force, and I worked as a Stationary Engineer. (p. 5, 23, 27)

6. *Dewick/Sawatsky/Hollis Family: John, Bernice, Kathy, Shawntel*

The Dewick and Sawatsky families have lived in Western Canada for many years. Bernice (p. 33, 44) and Kathy (p. 45) are retired educators. John (p. 41) is a retired electrician. Shawntel (p. 46) works for the Canadian Border Services Agency.

7. *Jack Donohue*

Jack is a student at Woodward Hill Elementary (p. 38)

8. *Ken Donohue*

Ken is a parent at Woodward Hill Elementary. (p. 80)

9. *Mona E*

I am the eldest of four children. I was born in Ethiopia of Egyptian parents. I was educated in a French Canadian Catholic school in Addis Ababa, and attended university in England. I emigrated to Canada in 1979. (p. 36)

10. Ghidaa

My name is Ghidaa. I am married and I have three boys. I was living in Mosul and we had to leave in 2014 because of ISIS. They took our homes, our land, and we were kicked out. We moved from Mosul in 2014, lived in Jordan for one year, and then we applied for United Nations refugee status. We came to Canada one year and two months ago and we are very grateful for life in Canada. We are very thankful because we never expected that we would be accepted here, and we are grateful to Canada. Thank you. (p. 32)

11. Karan Gill

Karan is a student at Woodward Hill Elementary. (p. 78)

12. Maggie Gooderham

I was born in England in 1923. I joined the British Air Force during WW II and served in Egypt. My first husband was an Air Force pilot who died in a plane crash. My second husband was a Canadian doctor who brought me to this country. (p. 14, 15, 17, 18)

13. Kahil Harji

Kahil is a student at Surrey Centre Elementary. (p. 38)

14. Joanne Harris

I was born in January 1929 in northern Saskatchewan, near Melfort. I was the youngest of 8 children. I left there at 17 to start a career as a secretary and steno in Winnipeg and Montreal. I came to Vancouver in 1961, where I met my husband. We married in 1966 and moved to Tsawwassen, where I still live. (p. 53, 84)

15. Nathanial Headley

Nathanial is a student at Woodward Hill Elementary. (p.74)

16. Dennis Horgan

I was born in County Cork, Ireland, but I grew up in Jersey in the Channel Islands during the German Occupation. My Dad was also born in Ireland, just after the potato famine.

In '57 Dad come out here to Canada, and they brought the 3 youngest kids with them. One of them was me, unfortunately.

We came right to Langley. (p. 22)

17. Trace Johnston

Trace is a student at Surrey Centre Elementary. (p. 77)

18. Jas Kooner

Ms. Kooner is a teacher at Woodward Hill Elementary. She was exceptionally supportive of the ElderStory project. (p. 81)

19. Ishan Kumar

Ishan is a student at Surrey Centre Elementary. (p. 80)

20. Nathan Kwok

Nathan is a student at Surrey Centre Elementary. (p. 76)

21. Bernadette Law

I was born in Hong Kong. My mother gave birth to four children, all girls, and I was the youngest. I came to Canada to study Art at university, and have lived in Alberta and British Columbia ever since. I am a member of the Surrey Seniors' Planning Table. (p. 55)

22. Jack Lillico

Jack is a magician, salesman, mechanic and denturist, among his other interests. Now retired, he lives in Tsawwassen. (p. 2, 52)

23. The Long Family: Sandy and Roberta, Gordon, Jamie

The Longs were brought up in the 1950s in Palling, a farming community about half way across the province between Prince Rupert and the Alberta border. Their father was a homesteader, logger, and log home builder. Their mother was a school and piano teacher. Sandy (p. 7, 9) is still logging and sawmilling in Prince George, Roberta (From Trail) is a retired high school and ESL teacher, Jamie (p. 5) is a carpenter living in Nanaimo and working in the Oil Patch, and Gordon (p. 3, 69, 73) has retired from teaching in Prince George to live in Tsawwassen and...edit this book.

24. Luz Lopezdee

I am a member of the Surrey Seniors' Planning Table. I come from the Philippines. I am here to tell a story to my grandchildren so that they will have a glimpse of their roots. (p. 50)

25. Dorothea Lowndes

Dorothea was born in Brazil. At 17, she married an English engineer and went to live in the various places around the world where his work took them. She raised three sons along the way, and now lives in Tsawwassen.
(p. 88, 90, 93, 98, 103, 107)

26. Graham Mallett

Graham is a retired teacher and university professor who comes from Australia. He married Leda 1971 and has two daughters. He now lives Tsawwassen.
He is a 4th degree black belt and chief instructor of the Tsawwassen Shotokan Karate Club. (p. 53)

27. Kartar Singh Meet

I was born in India in 1941. I was the eldest boy in a family of 7 children. My father was in the British Indian Army. (p. 87)

28. Jennifer Melville Roberts

I was born in 1930 in Sealchart, which is just outside of Sevenoaks, south of London. I came to Canada in 1956 and worked in bookkeeping and accounting until I retired and moved to Tsawwassen, where I live now. (p. 49)

29. Bernie Moon

My name is Bernie Moon from Korea, but actually I'm from the Philippines because I moved to the Philippines when I was forty-five. I lived there for ten years and came from there to Vancouver, because at the time my daughter was Grade 12 and preparing to go to university, so I thought the American educational system was much better than the Philippines. I chose UBC, so we moved here with two daughters and my wife, but I lost my wife about 10 years ago. Now I am remarried and living in Surrey and I am retired. (p. 39)

30. Mohammed Rafiq

My name is Mohammed Rafiq. I was born in India in 1945. My date of birth is not quite correct the way it has been written in my papers. Hardly anybody from those days has an accurate date. There are no records. Being busy in his job, my Dad sent us with somebody to go to school, and whatever the teacher wanted, he put as the date of birth.

My family migrated to Pakistan in 1949. My father was an overseer in the Irrigation Department in India. He had a very respectable job. When he migrated we had to leave everything in India and walk all the way to Pakistan.

Then in 1969 I immigrated to Canada. I was hired by the Ministry of Environment of British Columbia as an ecologist. I worked with them for almost 30 years and retired to Surrey in 2000. (p. 42, 76)

31. Mik Roberts

Mik is a student at Surrey Centre Elementary. (p. 85)

32. Joyce Schmalz

I was born in England in 1921, was in the British Military Police during the war, and came to Canada in 1946 as a war bride. I am an avid landscape gardener, and spend a lot of time on seniors' issues. (p. 13, 19)

33. Addison Shaw
Addi is a student at Surrey Centre Elementary. (p. 83)

34. Harprincevir Singh

Prince is a student at Surrey Centre Elementary.

35. Georgia Van De Bon

Georgia is a student at Surrey Centre Elementary. (p. 83)

36. Elaine Vaughan

Mrs. Vaughan is a teacher at Woodward Hill Elementary. She was exceptionally supportive of the ElderStory project and organized the storytelling classes there. (p. 79)

37. Elijah P. White

Eli is a student at Surrey Centre Elementary. (p. 85)

38. Cal Whitehead

I was born in Canada, in Vancouver. My parents had come down from the Rocky Mountain area of Cranbrook and married in 1923. (p. 48, 74)

39. Kendra Wilson

Kendra is a student at Surrey Centre Elementary.

40. Eeman Yousef

My name is Eeman Yousef, from Baghdad, Iraq. I left Iraq to go to live in Syria in 2007. I lived in Syria for nine years. I left because of the persecutions and wars. In 2014 in November I came to Canada. (p. 34)

41. Zong Quin Zhao

I come from China, where I graduated from University. Then I married and moved here to Canada. I began to learn English when I got here. Before I studied Russian in my university. But now I forget it all. (p. 40)

ElderStory Committee

Gordon A. Long

Gordon is the recording technician, storytelling coach and editor of the ElderStory Project. He was born and raised in Palling, a small farming community near Burns Lake, B. C. He is a retired teacher, a playwright, director and acting teacher, and the self-published author of 9 novels. He has been a member of the Planning Table since 2011.

Judith McBride

Judith is the administrator of the Planning Table and the ElderStory Project. She was born in South London, England in the winter of 1949. She moved to Canada in 1974, settling in B.C in 1976. She has worked for the last 40 years in charitable & nonprofit endeavours.

Chanchal Sidhu

Chanchal is the Manager of Multicultural and Community Programs at DIVERSEcity Community Resources Society. She oversees a diverse portfolio of programs from settlement and integration to food security and seniors' initiatives. She has been a member and supporter of the Surrey Seniors' Planning Table since 2013.

The ElderStory Project

This project was conceived by the Planning Table, supported by DIVERSEcity, and funded by the New Horizons for Seniors program of the Government of Canada.

First we held recording sessions, for individuals and groups of storytellers in KinVillage in Tsawwassen, DIVERSEcity offices in Surrey, in Langley Lodge and in people's homes.

A second part involved our storytelling coach giving workshops in Woodward Hill and Surrey Centre elementary schools. At an evening storytelling session students, teachers and parents were then invited to tell their family stories.

Now the stories have been transcribed and will be made into a series of books.

Surrey Seniors' Planning Table

The Surrey Seniors' Planning table is an organization of seniors dedicated to connecting seniors with the community. We accomplish projects involving multicultural and multigenerational cooperation and try to enhance the lives of Seniors and promote an age-friendly community.

Other Planning Table members in the ElderStory Project:

Beverly-Jean Brunet	Bernadette Law
Luz Lopezdee	Kay Noonan
Mohammed Rafiq	Roslyn Simon
Evelyn Wallenborn	

DIVERSEcity

DIVERSEcity Community Resources Society, established in 1978, is a not-for-profit agency offering a wide range of services and programs to the culturally diverse communities of the lower mainland. DIVERSEcity prides itself on its well-founded expertise in assisting immigrants and new Canadians in their integration into their new community. Our programs continue to expand and change to reflect the unique needs of the diverse community we serve. We have a strong commitment to raising awareness of the economic and cultural contributions immigrants make to Canadian society, and to raising awareness of the value of diversity.

New Horizons for Seniors

The New Horizons for Seniors Program is a federal Grants and Contributions program that supports projects led or inspired by seniors who make a difference in the lives of others and in their communities. By supporting a variety of opportunities for seniors, the New Horizons for Seniors Program works to better the lives of all Canadians. Since its creation in 2004, the Program has helped seniors lead and participate in activities across the country.

63596161R00072

Made in the USA
Lexington, KY
12 May 2017